FASHION
BEADING

FASHION
BEADING

Kim Ballor

05-993

Sterling Publishing Co., Inc.
New York

Prolific Impressions Production Staff:

Editor in Chief: Mickey Baskett
Copy Editor: Phyllis Mueller
Graphics: Dianne Miller, Karen Turpin
Styling: Lenos Key
Photography: Jerry Mucklow
Administration: Jim Baskett

Library of Congress Cataloging-in-Publication Data Available
Ballor, Kim, 1957-
  Fashion beading / Kim Ballor.
      p. cm.
  Includes index.
  ISBN 1-4027-1526-9
1. Beadwork. 2. Jewelry making. 3. Clothing and dress. I. Title.
  TT860.B328 2005
  745.58'2--dc22

                                          2004024486

10 9 8 7 6 5 4 3 2 1

Published by Sterling Publishing Co., Inc.
387 Park Avenue South, New York, N.Y. 10016

© 2005 by Prolific Impressions, Inc.
Produced by Prolific Impressions, Inc.
160 South Candler St., Decatur, GA 30030

Distributed in Canada by Sterling Publishing
c/o Canadian Manda Group, 165 Dufferin Street
Toronto , Ontario, Canada M6K 3H6

Distributed in Great Britain by Chrysalis Books Group PLC,
The Chrysalis Building, Bramley Road, London W10 6SP, England

Distributed in Australia by Capricorn Link (Australia) Pty. Ltd.
P.O. Box 704, Windsor, NSW 2756 Australia

Printed in China
All rights reserved
Sterling ISBN 1-4027-1526-9

About the Artist
Kim Ballor

Kim has spent nearly 20 years in the craft and creative industries as a designer, demonstrator, new product designer, teacher, author, and editor. She is the author of 18 art and craft instruction books, plus numerous published magazine articles in leading craft and hobby publications. She currently writes two magazine columns. She is a recognized professional educator with extensive on-camera and behind the scenes television experience.

Kim lives in beautiful Plymouth, Michigan and in her spare time, she finds therapeutic value in making her own lampwork beads. Find more of Kim's work at www.kimballor.com

Acknowledgements

My thanks to the **independently-owned bead stores** all over this country. In my travels, I have visited so many shops, sampled your wares, visited with you, and come away happy and counting my new beads! Special thanks to **Pam's Bead Garden** in Plymouth, Michigan (www.pamsbeadgarden.com) where I bought most of the beads used in this book. Thanks also to **Mickey Baskett and her staff** for making my book come to life.

A Note from Kim

I wrote this book for anyone with an interest in beading — whether you have beaded previously or are just now getting started in beading. Many of my acquaintances have learned the basic stringing techniques for making beaded jewelry and are now ready to move forward to something new. So I have included many designs with the basic stringing techniques for those beginner beaded jewelry makers. When you are ready to move on, I have included more advanced techniques. This book covers the tried and true material I teach in beading classes. Once you learn a couple of basic techniques, you will be able to build on and combine them to design projects with the beads you find and like. Start with a bead shopping spree and sit with this book to formulate your jewelry ideas. Enjoy yourself!

Kim

CONTENTS

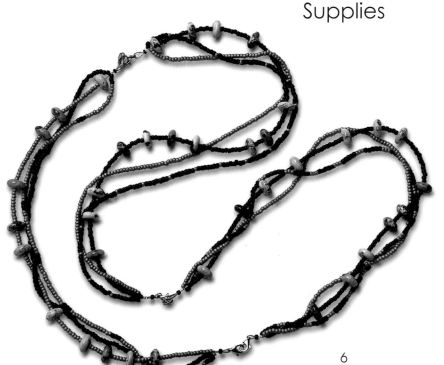

7

Beaded jewelry is intriguing - I love looking at the colors of the beads, and seeing how they move and shine in the light. The combinations of the textures of glass, metal, and crystal are fascinating.

This book teaches three easy basic beading techniques: stringing, wire loop wrapping, and stitching dangles and fringe. Basic color and design lessons with tips and ideas are explored. Easy-to-follow, step-by-step instructions with photos and illustrations are provided for each of the more than 50 projects.

Stringing, Wire Wrapping & Stitching: Why Not Start Today?

You'll find wonderful necklaces, bracelets, earrings, pendants, and watches, plus great ideas for embellishing clothing and accessories with beads.

With the growing popularity of beading, access to beautiful beads, tools, and findings has increased, so there's no reason not to try your hand at designing and making your own beaded jewelry. With these projects as examples, some basic tools and wire, and beads you like, you can create unique jewelry that displays your personality and causes your friends to say,

"Wow! I can't believe you made that!"

The projects in the book will provide you with ideas and inspiration, but I want to warn you. In an hour or two, you will have your first handmade necklace or bracelet, and you'll be hooked. And having a great time.

Making jewelry for yourself or making jewelry for gifts is easy and fun. Enjoy!

Kim Ballor

Birthstones

One way to honor a friend's birthday is to create a piece of jewelry featuring the person's birthstone or beads in the color of the birthstone. These are the ones most commonly designated for each month of the year, and descriptions of the stones are provided:

JANUARY - Garnet (deep blood red)

FEBRUARY - Amethyst (purple)

MARCH - Aquamarine (pale, watery blue)

APRIL - Diamond (clear)

MAY - Emerald (deep green)

JUNE - Alexandrite (lavender blue - but the real stone looks different in daylight and fluorescent light; imitations will look the same). Pearls are often used instead.

JULY - Ruby (bright red)

AUGUST - Peridot (pale green, often pale yellow-green)

SEPTEMBER - Sapphire (dark blue)

OCTOBER - Rose zircon (pink) or opal (multi-colored)

NOVEMBER - Topaz (The natural color is brown or smokey gray, but treated blue topaz is also popular.)

DECEMBER - Blue zircon (A brighter blue stone than aquamarine. Synthetics and imitations are often a bright turquoise blue.)

Design & Color Tips

You can follow the steps of the projects in this book with great results, but if you want to create original designs, knowing a few design principles is helpful. These are the same basic principles used by professional jewelry designers. Knowing these principles is specially helpful when you're trying to come up with a workable design solution.

Random vs. Pattern

These two necklaces were made with the same beads - obviously, the way you arrange the beads makes a difference in the way the necklace looks.

REPEATING PATTERN
Specific beads are placed at specific intervals.

RANDOM STRINGING
The beads are strung with no special order or pattern.

13

Symmetry vs. Asymmetry

These necklaces also were made with the same beads. The necklace made in a symmetrical design looks the same on each side of the center focal piece - one side is a mirror image of the other.

The asymmetrical necklace, even though it has the same beads, is different on each side of the center focal point. The sides don't match.

Focal Point

The focal point of a design is the bead or grouping of beads that stands out and first draws your attention. It may be in the center, or it may not. A piece of jewelry doesn't need to have a focal point, but you can see in the photo below how the addition of a focal point makes a very different bracelet.

Texture

Adding visual or tactile texture is a way to add interest - this bracelet has fibers added for texture. A bracelet made of bumpy beads would also have a lot of texture; another way to add texture is by adding fringe. (See the Techniques section for instructions on making bead fringe.)

Using a Color Wheel

A color wheel can help you select colors for beading. We learned in elementary school that the primary colors are red, blue, and yellow. Those colors are combined to create the secondary colors - green, orange, and purple. Continued combining yields additional colors.

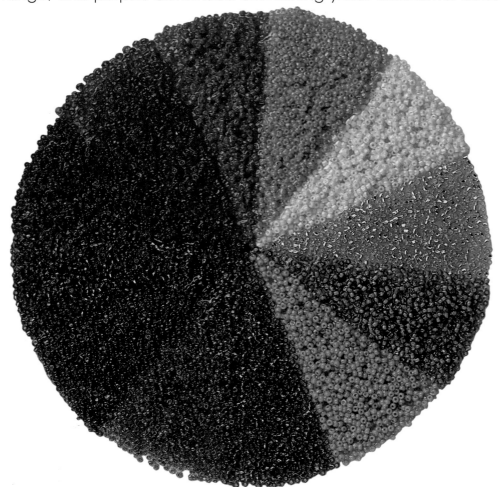

Basic color theory provides standard ways to use color. After you've chosen a color, the wheel can show you different color combinations. For this lesson, we start with one big blue bead and look to the color wheel for ideas.

MONOCHROMATIC COLOR SCHEME

A monochromatic color scheme uses only beads from the same color family - in this case, only shades and tints of blue.

COMPLEMENTARY COLOR SCHEME

For the complementary color scheme, start with blue and go directly across the color wheel to find the complementary color, orange. A complementary color scheme is energetic.

ANALOGOUS COLOR SCHEME

On the color wheel, analogous colors are next to each other. Analogous colors for blue are purples and greens. An analogous color scheme is calming.

*Three bracelets, **pictured left to right**, with analogous, complementary, and monochromatic color schemes.*

BEAD-STRINGING SUPPLIES

A few good tools, wire and cord, plus some lovely beads are what you will need to make beautiful necklaces, earring, pins, and embellished fashions.

The supplies are relatively small and few, so this craft is perfect to take with you wherever you go. Find a handy carrying case and you can create jewelry on the go.

Beads

Beads come in a huge variety of shapes, sizes, hole diameters, and materials. Shopping for and finding beads are fun parts of designing and making jewelry, and the popularity of beading has made beads available in almost every craft store and on the Internet. If you live near a bead store, you'll find everything you need in one stop. Or you may restring beads from an heirloom piece, an old bracelet, or a necklace you find at a yard sale. You can find bead artists at crafts shows or even commission custom beads from an artist's website.

Sometimes a bead or set of beads will catch your eye, and you'll just have to have it. A really great thing about making bead jewelry is that there is no rule about what kinds of beads or colors of beads go together. It's all up to you.

COLORATION TERMS

Iris beads are usually dark and opaque and have an iridescent coating.

AB (Aurora Borealis) are translucent beads with a pastel multi-colored coating.

Matte beads are not shiny and may have been chemically etched for a frosted look.

Ghost beads are translucent matte beads with an AB coating.

Transluscent beads are semi transparent. You can see through them, but not clearly.

Transparent beads, even when colored, transmit light and you can see through them.

Opaque beads transmit no light so you can't see through them.

Number of Round Beads for Common Strand Lengths

These numbers refer to unknotted strands. If you are using a clasp, subtract a few beads to accommodate the length of the clasp.

Bead Size	16"	20"	24"	36"
3mm	130	170	200	300
4mm	100	127	150	225
6mm	67	85	100	150
8mm	50	63	75	113
10mm	40	50	60	90

MEASURING BEADS

Beads are sized in millimeters or have size numbers. The size is the widest point on the outside of the bead (usually from one side of the hole to the other side).

They are sold individually (by the piece), by the strand, or by weight. A **mass** is the standard of measurement many bead manufacturers use, and wholesalers often offer a significant discount for whole masses of a single type of bead.

Types of Beads

Included with every project in this book, you will find information for the particular beads used and a description that includes the size so you can substitute other beads if you like. When selecting beads, check to see that they are colorfast (so they don't rub color on your clothing) and inspect the holes for rough edges or sharp points that could cut your wire or string.

GLASS BEADS

Pressed or molded beads come in all shapes, sizes, and colors. Some are smooth, some are faceted. Faceted ones are often referred to as "**crystals.**"

Lampwork beads are individually handcrafted glass beads that are made from glass rods that are melted with a torch. The hot glass is wrapped around a wire that, when removed, forms the bead's hole. The bead is heated in a kiln and allowed to cool slowly (this process is known as annealing). Lampwork beads are usually one of a kind and used as focal beads in designs.

Seed beads are small, short glass beads that are made from glass tubes, cut to length, then heated until smooth. Seed beads are sized by number, not millimeters. The smaller the number, the larger the bead. You will find them in sizes 6-15; sometimes labeled as 6/0, 8/0, 9/0, etc. The size 11 is a good, all-purpose size that is used extensively in these projects. Seed beads come in opaque, translucent, and transparent finishes and in round, triangle, hexagon, and square shapes. Most seed beads are made in Japan or The Czech Republic. Choose high-quality seed beads for best results. Poor quality seed beads have sharp ends while good quality beads have smooth ends. Good beads will not cut or fray your beading thread or wire,

Glass beads

making the larger investment worthwhile.

Bugle beads are long seed beads. They are made from glass tubes and cut longer. They can range in length from 5mm to 30mm. They are either smooth or twisted.

METAL BEADS

Metal varietal beads can be made of gold, silver, brass, copper, or mixed metals or may be plated over a base metal.

Bali silver beads are handmade sterling silver beads that come in a variety of shapes, sizes, and degrees of ornamentation. They are made in Bali and are 92.5% silver. The silver is melted and pressed onto a sheet of metal. Round shapes are punched out and hammered into a round hollow bead, then decorated. Bali beads will tarnish when exposed to air so keep jewelry in an airtight plastic bag. Polish with a polishing cloth but do not remove the oxidation that characterizes Bali silver.

Bali silver beads

GEMSTONE BEADS

Gemstone beads can be natural or manmade. They come in all colors - some natural, some dyed - and in many shapes. Natural gemstone beads are precious and semi-precious natural stones.

Opaque gemstones are those that light cannot pass through, such as pearls, turquoise, coral, malachite, and carnelian.

Translucent gemstones are somewhat clear, and light can pass through them. Examples include ruby, sapphire, aquamarine, and emerald.

Donuts are flat circular beads with center holes. They are often made from semi-precious stone, although other materials may be used.

Gemstones

POLYMER CLAY BEADS

Polymer clay beads are handmade from polymer (plastic) clay and baked in a home oven. They can be any size or shape. If you'd like to make your own polymer clay beads, you can read a book (there are a number available) or take a class. Polymer clay is available at crafts stores.

Polymer clay beads

Wire

There are different kinds of wire for different purposes, from thin and flexible to thicker with limited bendability. Wire is measured by gauge and designated by a number - the higher the gauge, the thinner the wire.

All wire should be cut with wire cutters. Cutting wire with scissors makes the scissors useless for cutting anything else.

BEAD STRINGING WIRE

When you string beads to make a piece of jewelry, you want it to be durable and unbreakable. It is best to string on wire instead of thread. Jewelry stringing wire is made by a variety of manufacturers, but is basically the same. It is made of woven strands of stainless steel wire that are coated in nylon. It is waterproof (so it won't rust or tarnish), flexible, and hypoallergenic. It comes in colors to coordinate with beads.

Wire comes in different diameters - the thicker the wire, the better the resistance to breaking and cutting. For pearls or seed beads, use a small diameter wire. A medium diameter will work for almost any jewelry project. Larger diameter wire is designed for items such as bracelets and watches that must withstand a lot of movement and bumping. It's also a good idea to use the largest diameter if you are stringing inexpensive, mass-produced beads. These beads usually have rough edges around the holes that can cut thinner wire. Projects in this book use size .14, .19, and .24mm beading wire. Manufacturers commonly refer to these as 014, 019 and 024 diameter wire.

You will need to match the diameter of your crimp tubes to the diameter of the wire. If you use a heavy wire, a larger diameter crimp tube will be needed.

STERLING SILVER WIRE

Sterling silver wire can be hard or soft, round, square, or half round. Lower gauge wire is thicker and stronger but harder to work. In this book, I used it for the wire-wrap technique.

You can also buy **silver plated wire** - it's less expensive than sterling silver but gives the same look. I also used **copper plated wire** on a few projects in this book.

Bead stringing wire

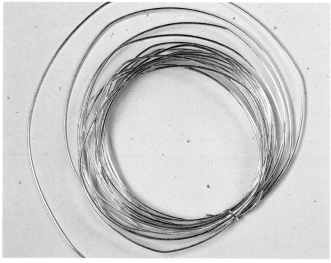

Silver wire

Thread & Cords

BEADING THREAD & NEEDLES

Beading thread is used for bead stitching and making fringe. It is made of strong twisted nylon to keep your work from breaking. Some threads should be waxed with **beeswax** or special **thread wax** to keep them from tangling as you work. There are some threads available that are pre-waxed. You will find beading thread in sizes, reflecting the diameter, on both bobbins and spools. Look for 0, A, B, C, and D, with D being the heaviest. You will almost always use size D in your beadwork. It will work for every project in this book that uses seed beads. Select the color of your beading thread to match the color of the beads you will be using. If you cannot match or you are using many colors of beads, select a neutral beige or gray thread. Unless you are using white beads, white thread will show a lot in your work.

Beading needles come in different lengths and are thin enough to go through even the smallest seed beads. Get out a good light and your magnifiers to help you thread these needles. The larger the number of needle, the smaller the diameter. Most beaders and bead projects work with a size 10 or 12 needle. This size needle will easily go through a size 11 seed bead. Beading needles vary in length from an inch to two inches. The longer needles are desired because you can load many beads at once when stringing them. However, because of their length, they bend while working. This does not hurt the process, but some beaders don't like it. You will try a few needles before you find the one that is perfect for you.

Needles for Seed Beads	
Bead Size	Needle Size
10 or larger	Size 10
11 and 12	Size 12
13 and 14	Size 13
15 and smaller	Size 15

OTHER TYPES OF CORD

Waxed linen cord works well for stringing most beads except seed and bugle beads. It knots well and can be used for necklaces that have beads up to the clasp.

Leather cord can be used to string pendants. It's easy to work with; **waxed cotton cord** is similar to leather cord but, being manmade, it is more regular in size and color than leather cord.

STRETCH ELASTIC

Stretch elastic cord can also used for stringing. It's great for adjustable jewelry like bracelets and for kids' jewelry. Elastic cord comes in colors and clear and in different diameters. Use the thickest diameter that will work with your beads and crimp tube.

Beading thread, needles, and thread wax

Stretch elastic

Jewelry Findings

Findings is the name given to the metal items that transform beads and wire into jewelry, such as **earring wires**, **pin backs**, **clasps, including toggle clasps**, **head pins**, **chain link charm bracelets**, **links**, and **jump rings**. Jewelry findings can be found in sterling silver and other metals.

Clasps: Choose clasps that are appropriate in size and style for the necklace or bracelet you are making. **Lobster clasps** are easy to see and operate. **Hook-and-eye** and **toggle clasp** sets may be inappropriate for delicate necklaces. You can also make your own - instructions and patterns are included in the Techniques section.

Crimp beads or tubes are small metal beads that you flatten with a **crimp tool** to hold clasps to the ends of your jewelry pieces. Crimp tubes come in different diameters (match them to the gauge of your beading wire) and in base metals and sterling silver.

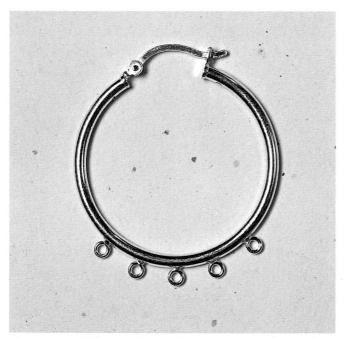

An earring finding with loops for attaching beads is called a chandelier finding.

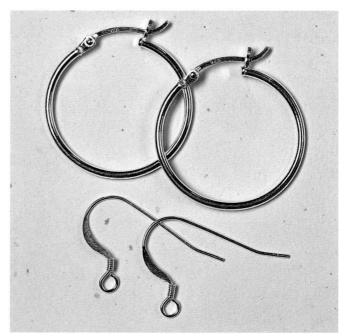

Two types of earring findings - loops and ear wires.

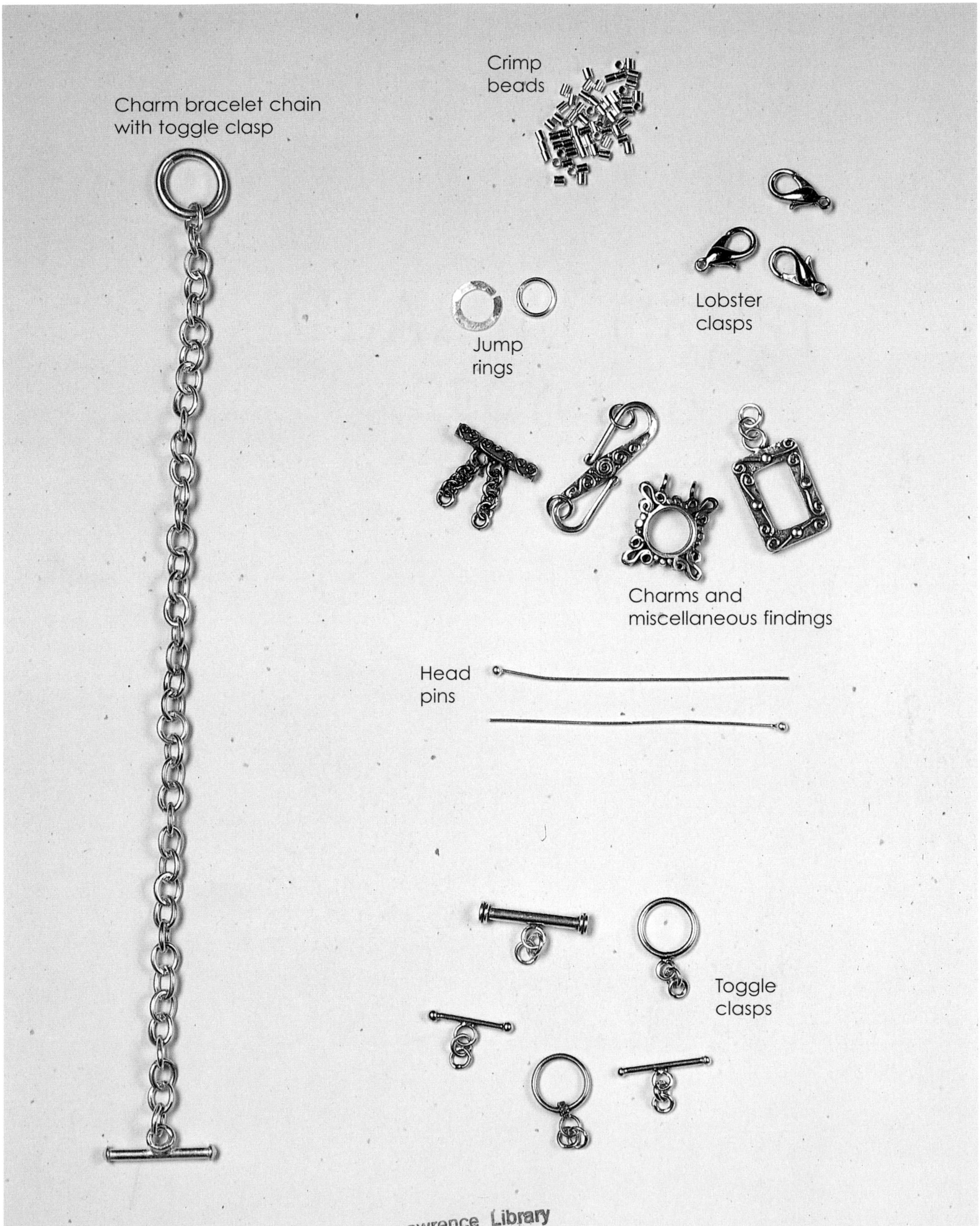

Charm bracelet chain
with toggle clasp

Crimp
beads

Jump
rings

Lobster
clasps

Charms and
miscellaneous findings

Head
pins

Toggle
clasps

Other Supplies

ADHESIVES

Beading glue is strong and flexible. Use it for securing knotted threads.

Epoxy adhesive and **silicone** adhesives are other good choices for jewelry making

RIBBONS & FIBERS

Ribbons, fibers, and cords add color and texture to your jewelry. You can use them for stringing, for fringe, or as strands - find them at fabric stores, knitting shops, and craft stores. Beads with larger holes are easier to use with ribbons, fibers, and cording.

OTHER HELPFUL TOOLS

Magnifying glasses are handy for threading beading needles and for working with small beads. A pair of good-quality **Tweezers** is helpful for picking up beads and untangling threads.

Measuring tape or ruler to accurately measure lengths needed for wire, thread, etc.

Beading tray or mat will give you a surface for holding your beads in compartments and is helpful when designing and string your beads. Many boards have measurements on them also. You could also use a small flat dish or pan. Avoid plastic as it will cause the seed beads to have static electricity and you will be chasing the beads around the tray. Some beaders prefer a soft, non-fuzzy fabric mat. Good tools always make the job easier.

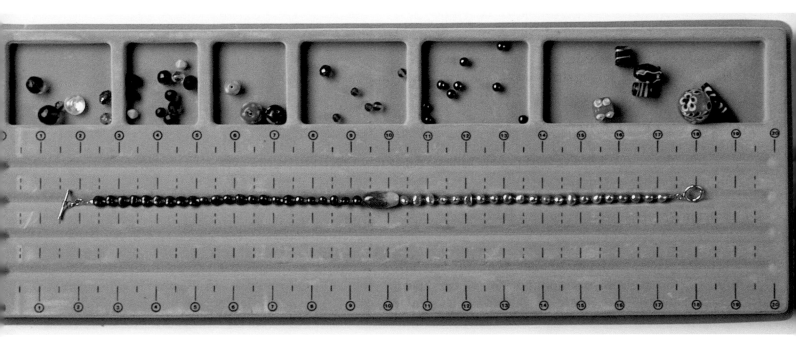

Beading Board

Tools

For the projects in this book, you need only a few tools, but having the right tool is important. Choose pliers and cutters with spring-loaded handles; they are much easier on your hands.

Side cutters are sharp wire cutters that are designed for close cutting - they don't leave sharp wire ends that will poke you when you wear your jewelry.

Round-nose pliers have smooth, round, tapered jaws. They are essential for making smooth wire wraps for dangles.

Chain-nose pliers have flat jaws and are used to grab and flatten. The best chain-nose pliers for making jewelry are smooth. Pliers with grippers might seem helpful, but they're not - they mar the wire.

Crimping tool has two holes on the jaw. Use it to close crimp tubes.

Scissors are needed for cutting thread - but don't use them on wire. Small sharp ones work best for delicate bead work.

Crimping tool

Pictured clockwise from top left: round-nose pliers, chain-nose pliers, crimping tool, side cutters.

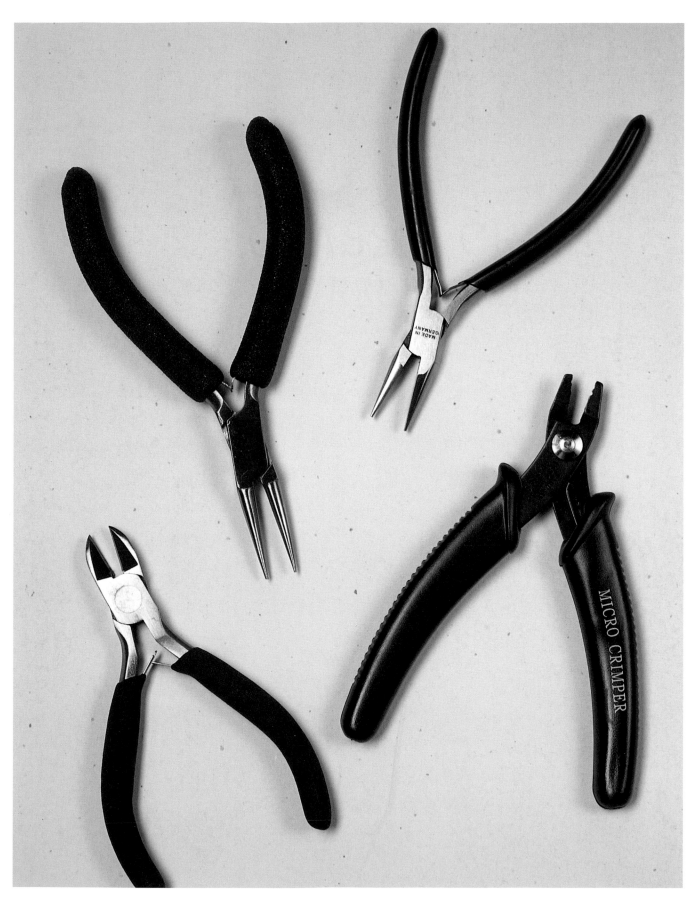

STRINGING TECHNIQUES

To string beads, all you have to know is how to attach a clasp. For this you will need a two-part clasp, two crimp tubes, and a crimping tool.

Making Your Own Toggle Clasps

It's easy to make your own artful toggle clasps. Any wire will work for this, but heavier wire is better. Hammering the metal makes it stronger.

You Will Need

Wire, 16 gauge or heavier
Side cutters
Roundnose pliers
Small anvil or bench block
Flat head hammer
Metal file

Hammer and Anvil

How to

1. Shape a piece of wire with an opening for a toggle bar to fit through. Include a small circle to attach to the jewelry piece.

2. Lay on anvil and hammer flat.

3. Tighten up the design and re-hammer.

4. Using roundnose pliers, shape a bar with a circle at the middle for attaching.

5. Flatten on anvil, being careful not to over-flatten the place where the wire overlaps itself - flattening a lot here can weaken the wire.

6. Trim the end of the bar so it is at least 1/4" longer than the opening it will fit through.

7. Smooth cut ends with metal file.

8. Attach to jewelry piece. ❑

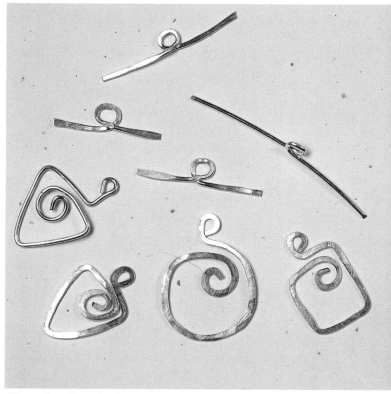

Examples of toggle clasps.

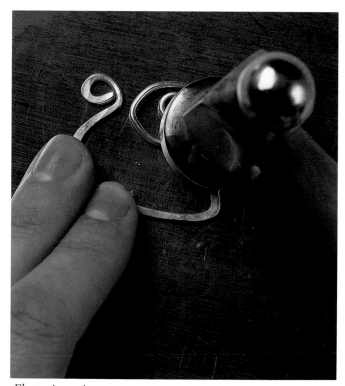

Flattening wire.

Patterns

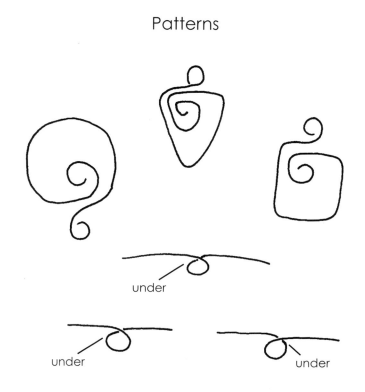

31

Attaching a Clasp
with a
Crimp Tube

You Will Need

Beading wire

Crimp tube

Small beads, such as seed beads

Clasp

Crimping tool

Optional: Chain-nose pliers

How To

FOLDED CRIMP:

1. On beading wire, string a crimp tube, a small bead, and the clasp piece.
2. Put the end of the wire back through the small bead and the crimp tube. Pull the end of the wire until there is just a small loop holding the clasp piece. (Photo 1)

Crimp beads holding clasp in place.

Photo 1 - Ready to crimp.

Photo 2 - Holding the crimp tube with the crimping tool to start a folded crimp.

3. Hold the crimp tube in the notch of the crimping tool closest to the handle. (Photo 2)
4. Separate the wires and squeeze firmly. (Photo 3) This folds the tube.
5. Move the crimp tube to the opening in the crimping tool tip. Squeeze the crimp tube to fold it in half. (Photo 4) This makes a folded crimp.

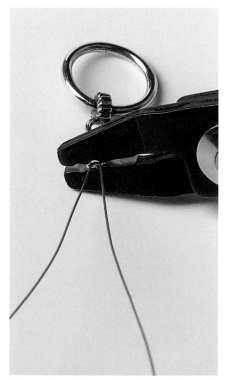

Photo 3 - Squeezing the crimp tube with the wires separated.

Photo 4 - Holding the crimp tube with the crimping tool before squeezing to make the fold.

Making Wire-Wrapped Loops

A wire-wrapped loop is better than a jump ring for holding dangles on a piece or for making connecting links of beads and/or wire. Once wrapped, the loop is completely secure.

It takes practice to do this neatly, and practice makes perfect loops.

How To:

1. With chain-nose pliers, bend the wire at a 90-degree angle, leaving a tail at least 1-1/2". (Photo 1) TIP: It helps to leave a longer wire tail - you'll have a better grip and better control of the wire.
2. Hold the wire on top of the bend with roundnose pliers. Using chain-nose pliers or your fingers, wrap the tail of the wire back over the round nose. (Photo 2)
3. Reposition the pliers so the lower jaw is in the curve. (Photo 3)
4. Bring the short wire under the bottom. (Photo 4)
5. Hold the loop flat in the pliers (You can use roundnose or chain-nose.) (Photo 5)
6. Wrap the tail around the base wire so the wraps touch each other. (Photo 6)
7. Trim the wire end with side cutters. Use chain-nose pliers to press the cut end flat against the base wire. (This keeps the cut end from snagging clothing or skin.) ❏

If you're worried that your wraps aren't perfect - don't be! When your jewelry piece comes together, the beads will stand out and your less-than-perfect wraps will be less noticeable.

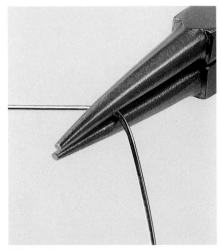

Photo 1

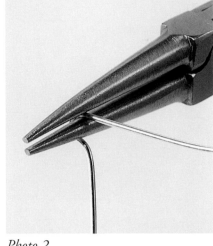

Photo 2

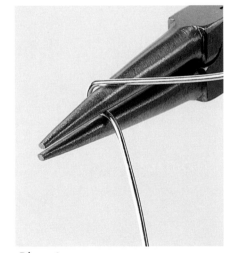

Photo 3

Photo 4

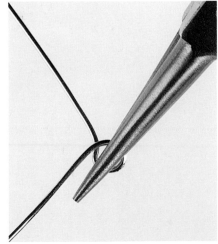

Photo 5

Photo 6

Stitching Fringe & Dangles

Bead fringe and dangles can be stitched to fabric or into
a base of strung beads.

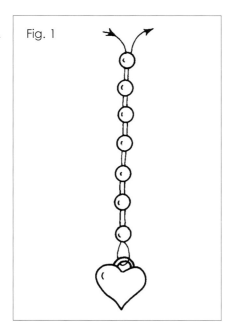

Fig. 1

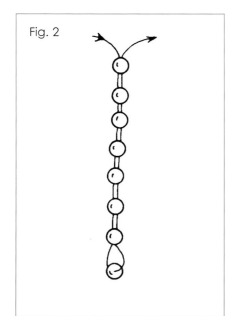

Fig. 2

Prepare:

1. Cut a piece of silk beading thread between one and two yards long.

2. Gently stretch the thread by pulling on it all the way down its length. (It is better to stretch it before you begin stitching than to have it stretch after your piece is finished.

3. Pull the stretched thread across wax while holding it with your thumb. Do this twice to be sure the thread is coated. This conditions the thread, so it tangles and breaks less.

4. Put thread through hole of needle.

Make a Charm Dangle:

You can use the same technique to add a special bead or group of beads at the end of a dangle.

1. String the beads you want for the dangle.

2. Stitch through the loop of the charm.

3. Stitch through all of the beads of the dangle in reverse. (Fig. 1)

Make Bead Fringe:

This is a simple fringe. More elaborate fringes appear in projects in the stitching section.

1. String all beads you want for the fringe.

2. Stitch through those beads in reverse, starting in the next to last bead of the fringe. Gently pull the thread so all beads touch. (Fig. 2)

Knot & Finish:

You'll need to knot the thread when you are finished or when the thread is too short to continue. This is done around the base wire.

1. Make a loop with the thread you have left, holding it behind the base wire.

2. Put the needle over the wire and through the loop. (This wraps the thread around the base wire.) Do this two or three times. Pull tight.

3. Put a small dot of glue on the knot. Let dry before continuing trimming. Trim thread with small sharp scissors. ❏

SIMPLE STRINGING PROJECTS

Stringing, the easiest technique for making bead jewelry, is nothing more than placing beads on a piece of wire and crimping findings to the ends. You need beads, beading wire, crimp tubes, and findings. Stringing a simple one-strand bracelet or necklace takes only minutes.

The projects in this section are variations of
stringing, from a quick single-strand bracelet to
lariats and multi-strand necklaces, watches,
belts, and more.

RED CRYSTAL & BALI SILVER

bracelet & earrings

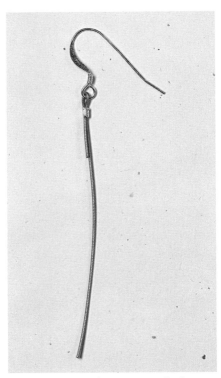

1. Wire crimped to earring finding.

2. Beads strung on the wire.

You Will Need

Beads, Wire & Findings:

Beading wire, .019 diameter

8 crimp tubes

Silver toggle clasp

2 silver earring wires

4 round red crystal glass beads, 12mm

20 red glass disc beads, 5mm

8 round Bali silver beads, 9mm

12 Bali silver spacer beads, 3mm

8 Bali silver disc spacer beads

8 Bali silver bead caps

Tools:

Side cutters

Crimping tool

Measuring tape

Follow These Steps

Make the Earrings:

1. Crimp a piece of wire to an ear wire. Trim wire tail as close to the crimp as possible. (photo 1)

2. String:
   red disc,
   round bali bead,
   another red disc. (photo 2)

3. Crimp a crimp tube on the wire about 12mm below the last disc. Trim the wire as close to the crimp tube as possible.

4. Repeat for second earring.

Make the Bracelet:

1. Cut piece of beading wire 2" longer than wrist measurement.

2. Crimp one piece of the toggle clasp to one end of wire. Trim excess wire.

3. String beads as follows:
   3mm spacer,
   spacer disc,
   3mm spacer,
   red disc,
   9mm bali round,
   red disc,
   bead cap,
   red crystal,
   bead cap,
   red disc. (photo 3)

4. Repeat pattern until bracelet is the right length.

5. Crimp remaining piece of toggle clasp to end. Trim excess wire.

6. Add a dangle to the loop of the circle end of the toggle clasp as a counterbalance for the bracelet: Crimp a piece of wire to the loop. String on a red disc, a round bali bead, and another red disc. Crimp a crimp tube on the wire under the last disc. Trim the wire as close to the crimp tube as possible. ❏

3. Bead pattern for bracelet.

TURQUOISE NUGGETS

necklace with clasp in front

You Will Need

Beads, Wire & Findings:

Beading wire, .019 diameter

4 silver crimp tubes

Decorative silver toggle clasp

18-21 turquoise gemstone nuggets, 10mm

51-60 black faceted glass disc beads, 3mm

1 large lampwork focal bead, 25mm

Tools:

Side cutters

Crimping tool

Measuring tape

Follow These Steps

1. Cut a piece of beading wire 2" longer than the desired length of necklace. Crimp one piece of the toggle clasp to one end of wire. Trim wire end.

2. String beads: 3 discs, then 1 turquoise nugget, repeating until desired length is reached.

3. Crimp remaining piece of toggle clasp to the end.

4. Cut a 4" piece of wire. Slide a crimp tube on one end. Crimp to open end of toggle clasp.

Closeup.

5. String one disc, the lampwork bead, and one disc. Crimp a tube right under the last disc. Trim wire as close to crimp tube as possible. ❏

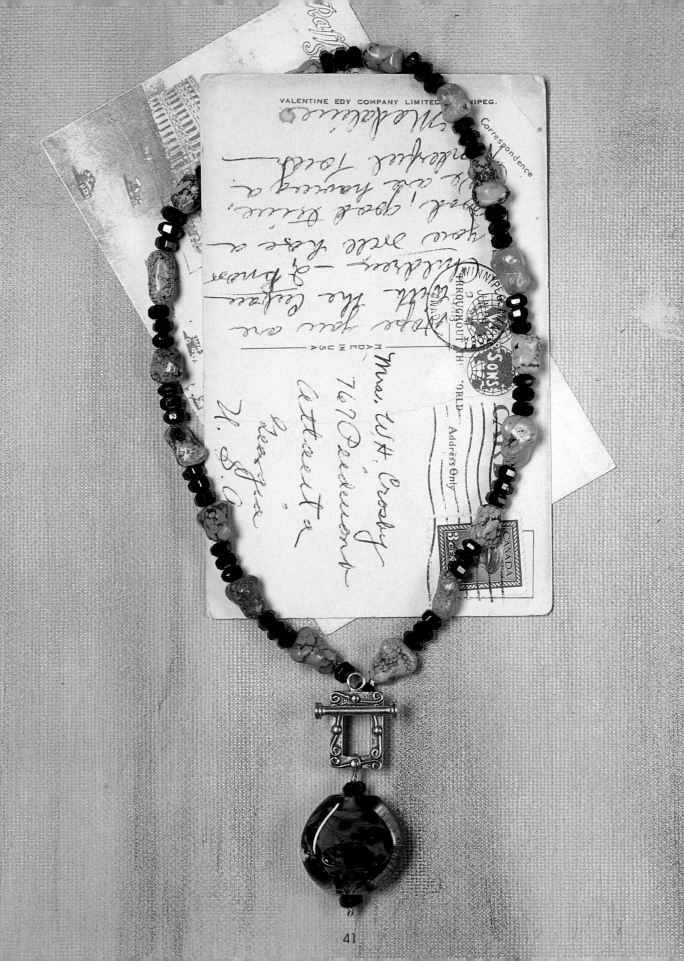

41

LEFTOVERS
lariat necklace

This necklace uses a "bead soup" of collected leftover beads - all sizes, all colors, all shapes.

You Will Need

Beads, Wire & Findings:

"Bead Soup" (assorted beads)

Beading wire, .019 diameter

8 silver crimp tubes

1 large lampwork focal bead, any size, in coordinating color(s)

Tools:

Side cutters

Crimping tool

Measuring tape

"Bead soup"

The beaded loop.

Follow These Steps

1. Cut a piece of wire 45" long.

2. String 4" of beads.

3. Slide a crimp tube over both ends of wire. Pull up tight to beads, making a loop and crimp. (See photo.) Trim short wire tail.

4. String beads to fill wire. When you have 4" of wire left, slide on a crimp tube and one large bead.

5. Bring the wire back through the large bead and the crimp tube. Pull snug, leaving a loop 1/2" long sticking out of the bead. Crimp.

6. Cut three pieces of wire about 4" each. Crimp each to the loop. Trim wire tails.

7. String beads on each wire, making them different lengths. Place crimp tubes close to the beads. Trim wires as close to the last beads as possible.

To wear the necklace long: Wrap around neck, put bead with dangles through loop.

Wear the necklace short: Wrap around neck twice, put bead with dangles through loop. ❑

MULTI-STRAND CRYSTALS

stretchy bracelet with ribbon tie

Use the same technique for stringing on wire to string an elastic bracelet. The number of beads you'll need depends on the size of your wrist.

You Will Need

Beads, Cord & Findings:
Clear elastic cord, 1mm
5 large diameter crimp tubes
Blue crystal cube beads, 4mm
Light blue crystal cube beads, 4mm
Crystal bi-cone beads, 5mm
Crystal round beads, 7mm

Other Supplies:
1/2 yd. white organza ribbon, 1-1/2" wide

Tools:
Scissors
Crimping tool
Measuring tape

Follow These Steps

1. Cut piece of elastic 3" longer than wrist measurement.
2. String bi-cone beads until long enough to go around wrist.
3. Slide crimp tube on elastic. Slide other end of elastic through crimp tube in the other direction. Pull ends of elastic until beads meet. TIP: If both ends of the elastic don't fit into the crimp tube, stretch one end of elastic as thin as you can and wrap around your finger, then push the other end into the tube.
4. Crimp the tube.
5. Repeat the process to make four more strands:
   • One strand with alternating bi-cones and rounds.
   • One strand with alternating light blue cubes and rounds.
   • One strand with a blue cube, 2 bi-cones. Repeat.
   • One strand with a round, blue cube, bi-cone, blue cube. Repeat.
6. Tie ribbon around all strands. Trim ribbon ends. ❑

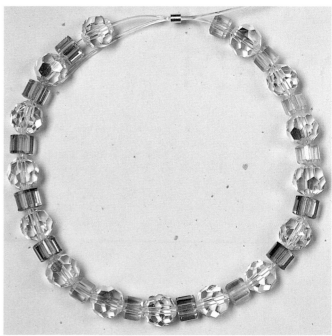

A single strand of the bracelet.

PERFECT TIMING
watch with beaded band

You Will Need

Beads, Wire & Findings:

Beading wire, .024 diameter

9 square lampwork beads, 1/2"

10 black glass spacer beads, 5mm

12 black opal bicone crystal beads, 7mm

8 black glass spacer beads, 4mm

Decorative silver toggle clasp

8-10 silver crimp tubes

Other Supplies:

Square or rectangular watch face

Tools:

Side cutters

Crimping tool

This flat-bead watchband watch looks great and wears well. You'll find many flat polymer clay beads in all shapes that work nicely for this design - choose spacers and crystals in colors to match the clay beads.

Follow These Steps

1. Attach two pieces of wire to each side of the watch face. NOTE: This watch has tube ends that wire fits into. Most watches have bars. If your watch has bars, crimp the wires to the bars.

2. On each side of watch, string one wire: lampwork square, crystal, big spacer. Repeat that pattern.

3. On the other wires, string: big spacer, crystal, lampwork square. Repeat that pattern.

4. Adjust wires to fit wrist, ending each wire with a bicone crystal. (This will make the watch lay nicely on the wrist.)

5. Crimp wires to the toggle clasp pieces with a crimp tube and a small black spacer.

6. Add a dangle to loop of the circle end of the toggle clasp as a counterbalance: Crimp a piece of wire to the loop. String on a spacer, a square, and another spacer. Crimp a crimp tube on the wire under the last spacer. Trim the wire as close to the crimp tube as possible. ❏

RIBBONS & BEADS
multi-strand necklace

You Will Need

Beads, Wire & Findings:

Beading wire, .014 diameter

12-15 assorted glass beads, 8-10mm

2 silver metal cones

14 silver crimp tubes

Size 11 seed beads - Hot pink, teal, blue

12" 20 gauge silver wire

Silver S-hook clasp

Other Supplies:

24" teal ribbon with flowers, 1-1/2" wide

24" hot pink organza ribbon, 7/8" wide

24" purple organza ribbon, 5/8" wide

24" black leather cord, 1mm

Tools:

Side cutters

Crimping tool

Round-nose pliers

Scissors

Measuring tape

Follow These Steps

1. Cut a piece of wire 24" long. String 18" of hot pink seed beads. Crimp the wire at each end of beads, centering the beads on the wire.

2. Repeat the process with blue seed beads.

3. Repeat the process with teal seed beads.

4. String four glass 8-10mm beads on wide ribbon. String three beads on hot pink ribbon. (photo 1) String three beads on purple ribbon. String each ribbon so beads are in different places. (You can adjust these when the necklace is finished.)

5. String three or four beads on leather cord. Tie a knot on each side of each bead to keep it in place. (photo 2)

6. Gather together one end of each strand. Cut 6" of silver wire and wrap around all strands tightly four to six times 2" from the ends. (photo 3) Trim all ends to 1/2".

7. Slide into the cone so the silver wire sticks out the narrow end and all ends are hidden inside the cone. (photo 4)

8. Twist, wind, and adjust all strands until all beads can be seen to the best advantage and the result pleases you.

9. Repeat step 6 with the other end of the necklace.

10. Wrap the exposed end of the silver wire on one end twice around roundnose pliers. Repeat on other end.

11. Slide one side of the silver S-hook on one loop. Slide the other side on the other loop. ❑

1. A bead on ribbon.

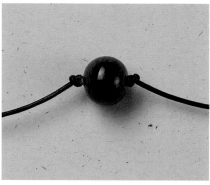

2. A bead on leather cord. The cord is knotted on either side of the bead.

3. The gathered strand ends wrapped with silver wire.

4. The end cone is added.

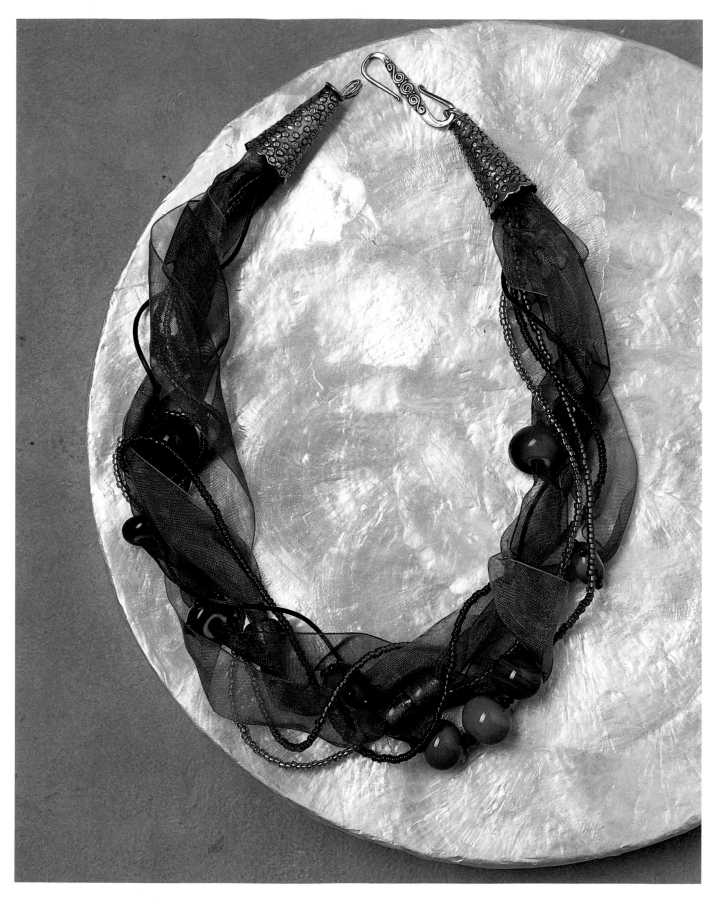

You Will Need

Beads, Wire & Findings:

Beading wire, .014 and .019

6 silver crimp tubes

6 silver lobster clasps, any size

1 strand yellow turquoise gemstone disc beads, 10mm

Black seed beads, size 8

Green seed beads, size 8

Tools:

Side cutters

Crimping tool

Measuring tape

Follow These Steps

Measure & Cut:

1. Measure around waist or hips - wherever you want belt to fit. Divide that measurement by 3. To that measurement, add 2".

2. Cut three pieces .019 beading wire that length. Cut six pieces of .014 beading wire the same length.

Make the Three Sections:

You are making three pieces that are virtually the same. When stringing the heavy wires, you can use a repeating

One part of a lobster clasp attached to wires.

WEAR IT THREE WAYS
belt or chokers

You can wear these pieces hooked together as a belt, wear one piece as a choker, or layer two or all three to make a striking necklace.

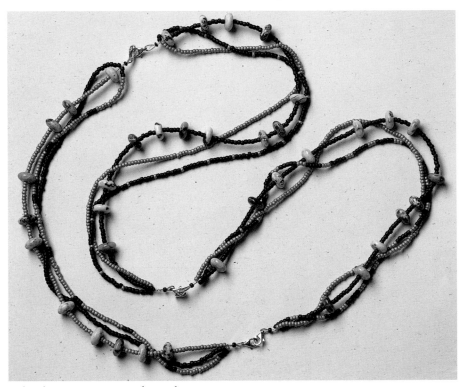

The three sections joined together.

pattern or random stringing. When stringing the thin wires with seed beads, you can string all one color or string a pattern using both colors.

1. Crimp a lobster clasp to the end of one piece of heavy wire and two pieces of thin wire. (See photo.)

2. On the heavy wire, string any combination of green seed beads or black seed beads with some turquoise discs.

3. On one thin wire, string black seed beads.

4. On the other thin wire, string green seed beads.

5. Crimp all three wires to another lobster clasp. See photo.

6. Repeat steps 1-4 to make two more pieces.

To wear as a belt, hook the lobster clasps of the three pieces together. ❑

CRYSTAL CUBES
bracelet & earrings

Crystal beads make beautiful dangle earrings. As they move and catch the light, they sparkle.

You Will Need

Beads, Wire & Findings:

Beading wire, .014

30 coral crystal cube beads, 4mm

31 fuchsia crystal cube beads, 4mm

9 orange round crystal beads, 9mm

Silver toggle clasp

8 silver crimp tubes

2 silver earring wires

Tools:

Side cutters

Crimping tool

Measuring tape

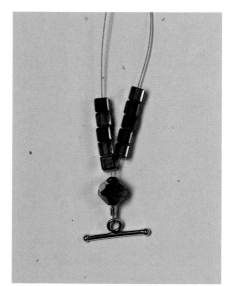

The beginning of one end of the bracelet.

Follow These Steps

Make the Bracelet:

1. Cut two pieces of wire 2" longer than wrist measurement. Holding them together, slip a crimp tube over both wires. Crimp to one end of toggle clasp.

2. Over both wires, string one round orange bead.

3. On one wire, string five cube beads, alternating colors.

4. On the other wire, string five cubes, but start with the other color. (See photo.)

5. String one round orange bead over both wires. Pull snug.

6. Repeat steps 2-4 until bracelet is desired length.

7. Crimp other end of toggle clasp to the bracelet.

8. Add a dangle to the loop on the circle end of the clasp as a counter-balance. Crimp a piece of wire to the loop. String on five cubes and a round orange bead. Crimp a crimp tube on the wire under the orange bead. Trim the wire as close to the crimp tube as possible.

Make the Earrings:

These are simple to make.

1. Crimp a piece of wire to an earring wire.

2. String five cube beads on wire, alternating colors.

3. Crimp at bottom of wire.

4. Repeat steps 1-3 to make a second earring. ❑

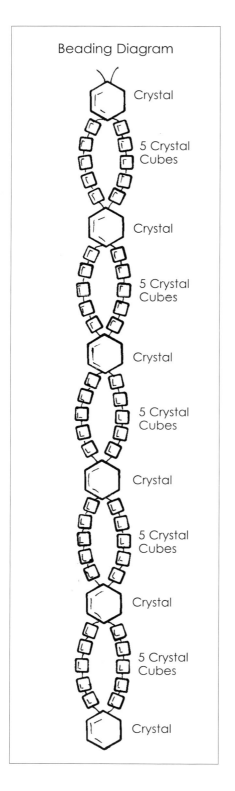

Beading Diagram

Crystal

5 Crystal Cubes

Crystal

5 Crystal Cubes

Crystal

5 Crystal Cubes

Crystal

5 Crystal Cubes

Crystal

5 Crystal Cubes

Crystal

PULSE ON PURPLE

two-strand necklace

This necklace is 18" long. For a longer necklace, add more beads and keep repeating the pattern.

You Will Need

Beads, Wire & Findings:

Beading wire, .014
19 fluorite gemstone beads, 10mm
90 purple oval crystal beads, 4mm
Purple seed beads, size 11
12 silver crimp tubes
Silver toggle clasp

Tools:

Side cutters
Crimping tool
Measuring tape

Follow These Steps

String the Necklace:

1. Cut two pieces of wire the desired length of necklace plus 4". (My necklace measures 18".)

2. Crimp both wires to one end of the toggle clasp.

3. Holding both wires together, string 15 crystals and 2 fluorite beads over both wires.

4. Separate wires. On top wire, string 9 crystals. On bottom wire, string 2" of seed beads (about 35).

5. String both wires through two fluorite beads.

6. Repeat the pattern until necklace is 3" shorter than desired finished length.

7. String 15 crystals over both wires.

8. Crimp other piece of toggle clasp to the end.

Add the Dangles:

The dangles hang between the pairs of fluorite beads.

1. Cut a 4" piece of wire. Crimp it between two fluorite beads.

2. String as follows:
   3 seed beads
   1 crystal
   3 seed beads
   1 fluorite bead.

3. Crimp wire close to the fluorite bead. Trim wire as close as possible.

4. Repeat the process to make four more dangles. ❑

DOUBLE TIME

watch or choker

This watch can also be a choker necklace - wear it either way! It's two pieces of jewelry in one.
To make sure the watch will fit, measure the wrist. The measurement of the watch face plus the strung wires should equal the wrist measurement. Lobster clasps come in many sizes. Select a size that will fit around your watch bar and rotate around it.

You Will Need

Beads, Wire & Findings:

Beading wire, .024

100 black and gold beads - all sizes, shapes, and materials

6-7 Bali silver beads, 8-10mm

2 silver charms

9 silver lobster claw clasps

20 silver crimp tubes

Other Supplies:

Round watch face

Tools:

Side cutters

Crimping tool

Measuring tape

Follow These Steps

1. Make the beaded strands by cutting three pieces of wire the length of the wrist measurement.

2. Crimp a wire to a lobster clasp. String beads on wire. Crimp other end to a lobster clasp.

3. Repeat the process for the other two strands.

4. Make a beaded dangle by cutting a piece of wire 4" long. Crimp wire to a lobster clasp. String 4-5 beads on wire. Crimp wire close to last bead.

The watch face with dangles attached.

The three beaded strands.

5. Make two dangles with charms by cutting two pieces of wire 4" long. Working one wire at a time, crimp wire to a lobster clasp. String:
4-5 beads,
a crimp tube,
a charm.
Slide end of wire back into crimp tube and crimp. Repeat to make second dangle.

6. Make six permanent watch dangles by cutting six pieces of wire 4" long. Working one wire at a time, crimp the wire to the watch bar. String 2-3 small beads. Crimp wire close to last bead. Place three dangles on each side of the watch.

To wear as a watch: Hook one end of each long beaded strand to one watch bar. Hook the other ends of the long beaded strands to the other watch bar around wrist. Hook dangles with lobster clasps to watch bars.

To wear as a necklace: Hook long beaded strands together. Hook the three dangles with lobster clasps on the lobster clasps at the ends of the beaded wires. Hook last lobster clasp around neck. ❑

Pictured at left: The choker.

PRETTY PEARLS

necklace

Traditionally, pearls are strung on heavy silk thread with knots between them so they don't rub against each other. (Pearls are soft, and rubbing can mar their luster.) My method (using seed beads between the pearls), while not the traditional way, is an easy way to string pearls that protects them as knotting does.

You Will Need

Beads, Wire & Findings:

Beading wire, .019

2 silver crimp tubes

Decorative silver toggle clasp

18-21 brown pearls, 6mm

18-21 pink pearls, 6mm

Crystal seed beads, size 11

1 brown and pink lampwork focal bead, 25mm

Tools:

Side cutters

Crimping tool

Roundnose pliers

Follow These Steps

1. Cut a piece of beading wire 4" longer than the desired length of necklace. Crimp one piece of toggle clasp to one end of wire. Trim wire end.

2. String pink pearls alternating with seed beads to the center of the wire.

3. Slide the lampwork bead on the wire.

4. Finish the choker by stringing brown pearls alternating with seed beads until the second side is the same length as the first.

5. Crimp remaining piece of toggle clasp to the end. ❑

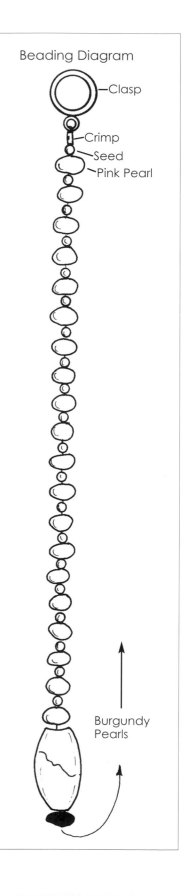

Beading Diagram

Clasp

Crimp

Seed

Pink Pearl

Burgundy Pearls

WIRE-WRAPPED LOOP JEWELRY PROJECTS

Wire wrapping is a durable way to add a bead
to a piece, and wire-wrapped dangles add
movement to your jewelry pieces. Once you
can wire wrap, you ll be making swingy, jingly
charm and dangle jewelry for everyone
you know!

Using the simple wire-wrap shown in the Techniques section, you can make dangles that look great on necklaces, bracelets, earrings, and more. Choose different beads for different fashion looks - elegant, fun, or artistic. For variation, try using colored wire or add the beaded dangles to findings you purchase at the bead or crafts store.

You can also use the wire-wrapping technique to make gorgeous earrings - all you need to do is make a pair and hang them from findings - and links for bracelets and necklaces.

TURQUOISE & SILVER
charm bracelet

An assortment of colorful beads are assembled on wires to make a series of dangle charms and attached to a link bracelet. TIP: Don't wire any beads within four links of the bar end of the toggle clasp - it makes the bracelet hard to get on if the beads are too close to the bar.

You Will Need

Beads, Wire & Findings:

Silver charm bracelet

20 gauge silver wire

7-8 turquoise polymer clay beads, 10mm

7-8 turquoise glass cube beads, 8mm

15-16 crystal bicone beads, 4mm

6-7 crystal rhinestone rondelles, 6mm

9-10 Bali silver flower charms

Tools:

Side cutters

Round-nose pliers

Chain-nose pliers

Follow These Steps

1. Count the number of links in your bracelet. From this number, subtract four. Divide this number by the number of polymer clay beads. This number is how many links should be between each polymer bead dangle.

2. Starting at link five from the toggle bar, wire the polymer beads to the bracelet. Include some crystal bicones on some of the polymer bead dangles.

3. Wire a turquoise cube and a flower charm between each polymer bead. Include some crystal bicones and some rhinestone rondelles in these dangles.

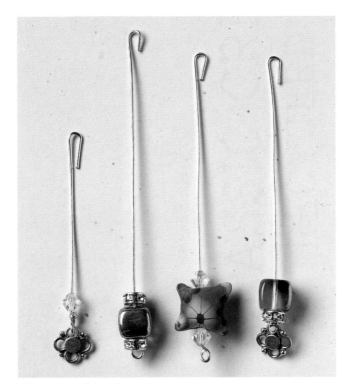

Examples of dangles

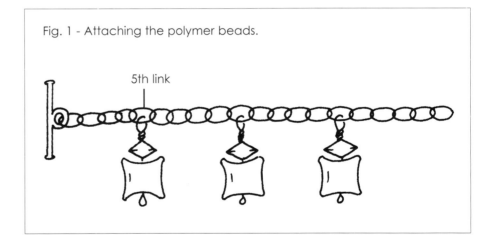

Fig. 1 - Attaching the polymer beads.

5th link

BUILD YOUR OWN
charm bracelet

The following pages show variations on the charm bracelet. Each bracelet was made by assembling a series of silver jump rings to make a chain, adding a toggle clasp, and decorating with beaded dangles.

When working with jump rings, it's better to open the ring by twisting the ends of the ring apart, not by pulling them away from each other. To add some strength to your chain bracelet, add a small dot of glue to the opening on each jump ring.

*Pictured at right, **top to bottom:** Butterflies Charm Bracelet, Black Crystals Charm Bracelet, and Silver Squares Charm Bracelet. Instructions begin on page 64.*

BUTTERFLIES
charm bracelet

You Will Need

Beads, Wire & Findings:
20 gauge silver wire
25-30 silver jump rings, 8mm
Silver toggle clasp
1 silver metal butterfly bead
2 silver metal butterfly charms
6 ice blue crystal beads, 4mm

Tools:
Side cutters
Round-nose pliers
Chain-nose pliers

Follow These Steps

1. Open one jump ring. Slide bar end of toggle clasp on jump ring. Close ring.

2. Open and add jump rings until your bracelet, including the other end of the toggle clasp, is long enough to fit the wrist.

3. Make three wire-wrapped dangles, using the butterfly charms and crystal beads.

4. Add the three wire-wrapped dangles to the link before the open end of the toggle clasp. ❑

SILVER SQUARES
charm bracelet

You Will Need

Beads, Wire & Findings:
20 gauge silver wire
35-40 silver jump rings, 8mm
Silver toggle clasp
6 square Bali silver beads, 13mm
6 bali silver swirl charms, 9mm

Tools:
Side cutters
Round-nose pliers
Chain-nose pliers
Anvil and chasing hammer

Follow These Steps

1. Lay a jump ring on the anvil. Hit with hammer until flattened. Flatten 12-13 jump rings.

2. Open one flattened jump ring. Slide bar end of toggle clasp on jump ring. Close ring.

3. Attach two non-flattened jump rings to the flat jump ring.

4. Repeat the pattern until the bracelet, including the open end of the toggle clasp, is long enough to fit the wrist.

5. Make wire-wrapped dangles with the square beads and swirl charms.

6. Hang the dangles, alternating the squares and swirls, from the pairs of un-flattened jump rings. ❑

BLACK CRYSTALS

charm bracelet

You Will Need

Beads, Wire & Findings:

20 gauge silver wire

25-30 silver jump rings, 8mm

Silver toggle clasp

25-30 black seed beads, size 8

25-30 black AB crystal beads, 6mm

Tools:

Side cutters

Round-nose pliers

Chain-nose pliers

Follow These Steps

1. Open one jump ring. Slide one seed bead and the bar end of the toggle clasp on jump ring. Close ring.

2. Open and add jump rings, each with a seed bead, until your bracelet, including the other end of the toggle clasp, is long enough to fit the wrist.

3. Wire wrap one crystal bead to each bracelet link. ❏

CRYSTAL CHANDELIER

Earrings

You can make your hoop earrings fuller by wiring more than one dangle to each loop.

You Will Need

Beads, Wire & Findings:

28 gauge wire

2 silver chandelier earring findings

2 silver fishhook earring findings

3 round clear crystal beads, 4mm *for each loop* on your findings

Crystal seed beads, size 11

Tools:

Side cutters

Round-nose pliers

Chain-nose pliers

Follow These Steps

1. Cut a 4" piece of wire. Wrap one end in a tight circle on the tip of the round nose pliers.

2. String as follows:
crystal,
seed bead,
crystal,
seed bead,
crystal,
5 seed beads.

3. Wire wrap a loop on the chandelier finding.

4. Repeat steps 1 through 3 for all loops on chandelier earring finding.

5. Repeat to make other earring.

6. Wire wrap each chandelier finding to a fishhook earring finding. ❏

LONG LINKS

bracelet

Wire-wrapped dangles are joined to create this bracelet.
Mine has beads in a variety of colors - you could choose to use
all one color, or two, or three. For a less bold, more elegant look,
use crystal bicone beads instead of rhinestone rondelles.

This bracelet is 9" long - it's a longer-than-normal length because
it doesn't bend the usual way. If you need to shorten this
bracelet to fit a small wrist, make each link shorter.

You Will Need

Beads, Wire & Findings:

18 gauge silver wire

6 glass beads in pastel colors, 5mm

10 rhinestone rondelles, 6mm

Silver toggle clasp

Tools:

Side cutters

Round-nose pliers

Chain-nose pliers

Measuring tape

Follow These Steps

1. Cut six pieces of wire, each 4" long. If the wire came in a coil, straighten the pieces.

2. Wrap the end of one wire to the bar end of toggle clasp.

3. Slide on the wire:
   rondelle,
   glass bead,
   rondelle.

4. Wrap a loop on the other end of wire, leaving the wire 1-1/2" long from end of loop to end of loop.

5. Wire wrap next piece of wire to the first. Add beads. Wrap a loop at end.

6. Repeat the process to make four more long links. Try to keep them the same length.

7. Add the open end of the toggle clasp and wire wrap the last loop. ❏

One long link.

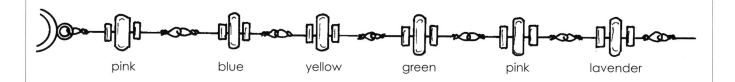

Fig. 1 - Long links connected

| pink | blue | yellow | green | pink | lavender |

RARE BLUE CORAL

bead necklace

This necklace is 18" long. Add additional bead links to make a longer necklace. The clasp is flattened wire you make yourself.

You Will Need

Beads, Wire & Findings:

20 gauge silver wire

16 gauge silver wire

15 round blue coral beads, 14mm

30 Bali silver bead caps

Tools:

Side cutters

Round-nose pliers

Chain-nose pliers

Metal file

Anvil and chasing hammer

Follow These Steps

Make Clasp:

1. Cut two pieces of 16 gauge wire, one 1-1/2" long and one 6" long.

2. Make a toggle clasp with the two pieces of wire.

3. Flatten with hammer on anvil. (photo 1)

Make the Links:

1. Cut 15 pieces of wire, each 4".

2. Make a wrapped loop at one end of the first wire.

3. Slide on the wire:
   bead cap,
   blue coral bead,
   bead cap.

4. Wrap other end of wire so the caps are tight to the bead. (photo 2)

5. Make more wire-wrapped links with the same bead pattern until all 15 links are complete, joining the links as you go.

6. Use the wire-wrap technique to make two 20 gauge wire loops to attach the toggle clasp pieces to the ends of the necklace. ❑

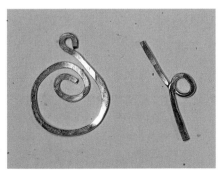

1. The pieces of the clasp.

2. One of the wire-wrapped beaded links.

69

LAMPWORK ADORNMENTS

necklace & bracelet

Round lampwork beads are complemented with an assortment of coordinating beads, including crystals in various sizes and shapes, rhinestone rondelles, seed beads, and bali silver rounds, spacers, and bead caps. Look for silver beads in unusual shapes and interesting bead caps that will add interest and texture.

BRACELET

You Will Need

Beads, Wire & Findings:

20 gauge silver wire

7 round turquoise green lampwork beads, 18mm

40 assorted coordinating beads

4 or 5 silver charms

Silver toggle clasp

Tools:

Side cutters

Round-nose pliers

Chain-nose pliers

Measuring tape

Follow These Steps

1. Cut a piece of wire 4" long. Wrap it to the open end of the toggle clasp.

2. Slide one large lampwork bead on the wire. Wrap the other end of the wire close to the bead.

3. Add the rest of the lampwork beads, wrapping each one to the link before it. Add bead caps on either side of the lampwork bead on one or two links.

4. Add three spacer beads and the bar end of the toggle clasp, then wrap the last loop. (The spacer beads make it easier to operate the toggle clasp.)

5. Make dangles of all kinds, combining the assortment of beads you have gathered.

6. Wire wrap three to four dangles to the loops between the lampwork beads.

7. Add charms as desired. ❑

NECKLACE

You Will Need

Beads, Wire & Findings:

20 gauge silver wire

9 round green lampwork beads, 18mm

8 round green lampwork beads, 12mm

75-80 assorted beads

3 or 4 silver charms

Silver toggle clasp

Tools:

Side cutters

Round-nose pliers

Chain-nose pliers

Follow These Steps

1. Cut a piece of wire 4" long. Wrap it to the open end of the toggle clasp.

2. Slide one large lampwork bead on the wire. Wrap the other end of the wire close to the bead.

3. Use a combination of large and small lampwork beads to make the links, wrapping each one to the link before it. Add bead caps on either side of the lampwork bead on one or two links. To add interest, try making a link or two with large crystal beads. Make the necklace 18-22" long, as you prefer.

4. Add the bar end of the toggle clasp, then wrap the last loop.

5. Make dangles of all kinds, combining the assortment of beads you have gathered.

6. Wire wrap three to four dangles to the loops between the lampwork beads. For comfort, don't add dangles where the necklace will rest on the back of the neck.

7. Add charms as desired. ❑

CHARMING BOTTLE CAPS
charm bracelet

Don't throw those bottle caps away - recycle!
Bottle caps make charming and nostalgic decorations for
a charm bracelet. These have photos glued inside them.

You Will Need

Beads, Wire & Findings:

18 gauge silver wire

4 square green lampwork beads, 16mm

Green seed beads, size 15

A few tiny green crystal beads

Silver charm bracelet chain

Other Supplies:

3 bottle caps

Small photocopied photos

Clear dimensional finish

Tools:

Side cutters

Round-nose pliers

Chain-nose pliers

Scissors

Drill with 1/16" bit

Follow These Steps

Decorate the Bottle Caps:

1. Drill a hole in the edge of each bottle cap (this will be the top). (Photo 1)

2. Cut photocopies to fit inside bottle caps.

3. Working one cap at a time, squeeze a little clear dimensional finish into the bottle cap. (Photo 2)

4. Lay cutout photocopy on top. (Photo 3)

5. Cover paper with dimensional finish. (Photo 4)

6. Repeat steps 3 through 5 for remaining bottle caps. Let dry.

1. Bottle cap with drilled hole.

2. Squeezing dimensional finish in the bottle cap.

3. Placing the photocopy in the bottle cap.

4. Covering the picture with dimensional finish.

7. Squeeze some dimensional finish around the bottom and one side inside each bottle cap. Sprinkle seed beads and crystal beads on the finish while wet. Let dry.

Assemble the Bracelet:

1. Count the links on the bracelet. Divide by seven. (This is the number of links you will skip between charms.)

2. Starting on the first link next to the open end of the toggle clasp, attach a wire-wrapped bead dangle. Continue wire wrapping, alternating bottle caps and beads until all seven pieces are attached to the bracelet. ❏

TURQUOISE & CROSSES
necklace

This necklace showcases the variety of colors of natural turquoise nugget beads and different-shaped silver cross charms. This necklace is 24". To make it longer, use a longer chain and more turquoise nuggets.

You Will Need

Beads, Wire & Findings:

20 gauge silver wire

12" silver chain with large links

8-9 turquoise nugget gemstone beads, 20mm

7-8 round Bali silver beads, 10mm

5 silver cross charms

Silver toggle clasp

Tools:

Side cutters

Round-nose pliers

Chain-nose pliers

Measuring tape

Follow These Steps

1. Cut piece of wire 4" long. Wrap a loop at one end. Slide a turquoise nugget on the wire. Wrap the other end of the wire up tight to the bead. (Fig. 1)

2. Add links of turquoise nuggets and round bali beads until your piece is 10-12" long.

3. Attach bar end of toggle clasp to one end of the chain. Wrap the other piece of the clasp to one end of the beaded section.

4. Cut a piece of wire 5" long. Wrap a loop at one end. Slide a turquoise nugget and a bali bead on the wire. Slide wire through the bottom loops of both the beaded section and the chain. Wrap. (Fig. 2)

5. Add another dangle at the bottom made with a cross charm and a bali bead.

6. Try on the necklace to determine where you wish to place the dangles on the chain. Wire wrap dangles of bali beads and cross charms on the chain. ❏

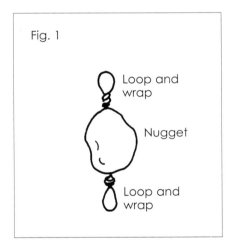

Fig. 1

Loop and wrap

Nugget

Loop and wrap

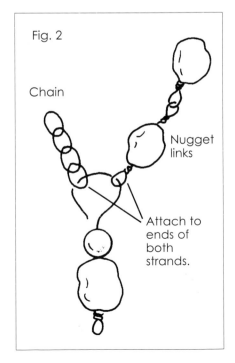

Fig. 2

Chain

Nugget links

Attach to ends of both strands.

HEART OF FASHION
wire-wrapped bangle bracelet

A single lampwork bead is the focal point of this decorated bangle.

You Will Need

Beads, Wire & Findings:

Silver bangle bracelet chain

18 gauge silver wire

Heart-shaped lampwork bead,
  28mm

2 crystal bicone beads, 4mm

1 rhinestone rondelle bead, 6mm

Tools:

Side cutters

Round-nose pliers

Measuring tape

Follow These Steps

Wrap the Bracelet:

1. Cut a piece of wire 18" long.
   Hold 1" of the end of the wire
   against the back of the bracelet.
   (Fig. 1)

2. Wrap the wire tightly around the
   bracelet, making a wrapped section about 7/8" long. (Fig. 2)
   When you have wrapped all but
   about 1/2" of the wire, bend it to
   the back and slide it under the
   wrapped wire. (Fig. 3) Using
   chain-nose pliers, pinch the end
   of the wire tightly to the back of
   the bracelet.

3. Repeat two more times, spacing
   the wrapped sections evenly
   around the bangle.

Make a Dangle:

1. Cut a piece of wire 8" long.

2. Make a dangle:
   bicone,
   rondelle,
   heart bead,
   bicone.

3. Wrap the dangle to the bracelet.
   ❏

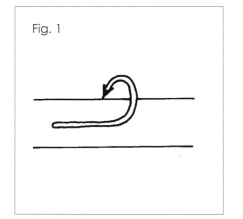

Fig. 1

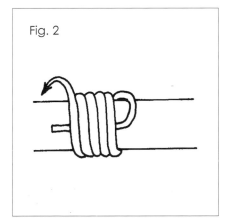

Fig. 2

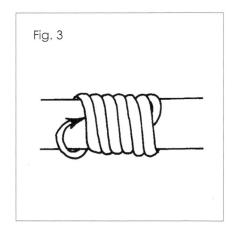

Fig. 3

PENDANT ON A CORD

bracelet

Make the same kind of dangle you made for the
Heart of Fashion bracelet from a crystal bead,
a rhinestone rondelle, and a square lampwork bead,
then hang it on a crocheted rope bracelet that
you purchase or make yourself. Just roll the
bracelet over your wrist to wear.

POLKA DOT BEADS

ear-wire earrings

You Will Need

Beads, Wire & Findings:

18 gauge silver wire

2 round lampwork beads with dots, 15mm

2 rhinestone rondelles, 6mm

2 bicone clear crystal beads, 6mm

2 wide bicone clear crystal beads, 8mm

2 silver ear wires

Tools:

Side cutters

Round-nose pliers

Chain-nose pliers

Follow These Steps

1. Wire wrap a dangle, stringing beads on wire as follows:
   small bicone,
   rondelle,
   lampwork bead,
   large rondelle.

2. Repeat to make other earring. ❏

CLAY BEADS ON HOOPS

earrings

You Will Need

Beads, Wire & Findings:

18 gauge silver wire

2 lentil-shaped purple/pink/red
   polymer clay beads, 18mm

2 purple cube crystal beads, 8mm

2 silver hoop earring findings,
   1" diameter

Tools:

Side cutters

Round-nose pliers

Chain-nose pliers

Follow These Steps

1. Wire wrap a dangle with a cube and a clay bead.

2. Repeat for other earring.

3. Slip each dangle over a hoop. ❏

CRYSTAL DROPS

ear-wire earrings

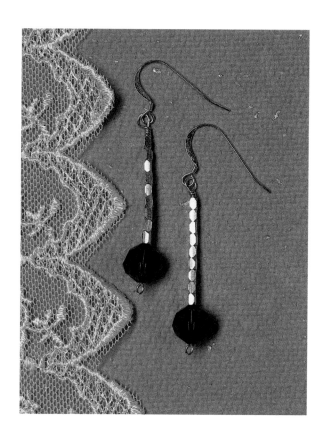

You Will Need

Beads, Wire & Findings:

24 gauge silver wire

2 round fuchsia crystal beads, 8mm

18 cut silver tube beads, 3mm

2 silver ear wires

Tools:

Side cutters

Round-nose pliers

Chain-nose pliers

Follow These Steps

1. Wire wrap a dangle with a crystal bead and nine cut silver beads to an ear wire.

2. Repeat to make other earring. ❑

CLAY FLOWERS
earrings

You Will Need

Beads, Wire & Findings:

20 gauge silver wire

2 red flower-motif polymer clay
beads, 12mm

4 green leaf-shaped polymer clay
beads, 10mm

30 green seed beads, size 11

2 silver ear wires

Tools:

Side cutters

Round-nose pliers

Chain-nose pliers

Follow These Steps

1. Wire wrap a dangle, stringing the following beads:
   5 seed beads,
   leaf bead,
   5 seed beads,
   leaf bead,
   5 seed beads,
   flower bead.
   Attach to ear wire.

2. Repeat to make other earring. ❏

TURQUOISE CRYSTALS
hoop earrings

It's easy to make these sparkly dangle earrings when you start with hoops that have loops for attaching the dangles. If you like, you can make your earrings fuller by wiring more than one beaded dangle to each loop.

You Will Need

Beads, Wire & Findings:

24 gauge silver wire

10 oval turquoise crystal beads, 8mm

20 silver and black metal disc beads, 3mm

2 silver earring hoop findings with 5 loops

Tools:

Side cutters

Round-nose pliers

Chain-nose pliers

Follow These Steps

1. Wire wrap a dangle on each loop with beads in this order:
   disc,
   crystal,
   disc.
   Place the black sides of the discs next to the crystal beads.

2. Repeat to make other earring. ❏

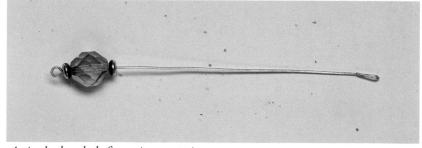

A single dangle before wire wrapping.

83

NATURAL STONE

buttons

Beaded buttons are easy to make and fun to wear. As buttons, these semi-precious stone beads add earthy elegance to a sweater or jacket.

To attach them, purchase some button pins at your local fabric store. Button pins are similar to safety pins - they allow you to temporarily attach buttons to a garment and remove them for washing or dry cleaning.

You Will Need

Beads, Wire & Findings:

For each button

1 polished semi-precious gemstone disc bead, 20mm

1 black glass disc bead, 6mm

1 smooth silver bead cap, 3mm

1 silver head pin with dangles

Option: If you can't find head pins with dangles, use 20 gauge silver wire, a small jump ring, and two tiny silver charms. Assemble the head pin yourself before assembling the button.

Tools:

Side cutters

Round-nose pliers

Chain-nose pliers

Supplies for one button.

Follow These Steps

1. Slide beads on head pin as follows:
   bead cap,
   black disc,
   turquoise bead.
   Wrap a loop tightly behind turquoise bead. Make **no more than** two wraps - more wraps will make the button hang forward when it is attached to the garment.

2. Repeat to make additional buttons. ❏

PINK SHELL
buttons

A fancy silver toggle clasp with leaves and swirls was the inspiration for these buttons. One part of the toggle clasp is sandwiched between a faceted crystal bead and a shell donut bead for a one-of-a-kind button that's sure to get noticed.

Attach them with button pins so they can be removed for washing or dry cleaning.

You Will Need

Beads, Wire & Findings:

For each button

Silver wire, 18 gauge

1 pink shell donut bead, 30mm

1 fuchsia crystal bead, 10mm

1 silver toggle clasp

1 disc bead with small center hole, any color (This will not show.)

Tools:

Side cutters

Round-nose pliers

Chain-nose pliers

Measuring tape

Supplies for one button.

Follow These Steps

1. Using side cutters, cut the loop off the back of the open end of the silver toggle clasp.

2. Cut a 6" piece of wire. Wrap a tight loop at the end of the wire.

3. String on wire as follows:

   fuchsia bead,

   silver toggle clasp,

   shell donut,

   disc.

4. Wrap a loop tightly behind the disc bead. Make **no more than** two wraps - more will make the shank too long.

5. Repeat to make additional buttons. ❏

FRAMED PHOTO
pendant necklace

The paper frame from a 35mm slide becomes the beaded frame for a small picture. This picture is from a deck of art print cards I bought in a museum shop.

You Will Need

Beads, Wire & Findings:
Silver wire, 18 gauge, 24 gauge
Light gold seed beads, size 11
5 gold glass beads, 5mm to 8mm
Chain *or* cord

Other Supplies:
Old 35mm photo slide with paper
    frame
Photo, old postcard, *or* art print, etc
Gold inkpad
Clear dimensional adhesive

Tools:
Side cutters
Round-nose pliers
Chain-nose pliers
Scissors
Glue of your choice
Small nail *or* awl
Measuring tape

Follow These Steps

Prepare the Frame:

1. Remove film from slide frame. (You can push it out to take the two halves of the frame apart and remove the film.) (photo 1)

2. Using the nail, poke a hole in the center top and the center bottom of the slide frame. (photo 2)

3. Pat gold inkpad over the front of the slide frame to cover the frame with ink.

Continued on page 90

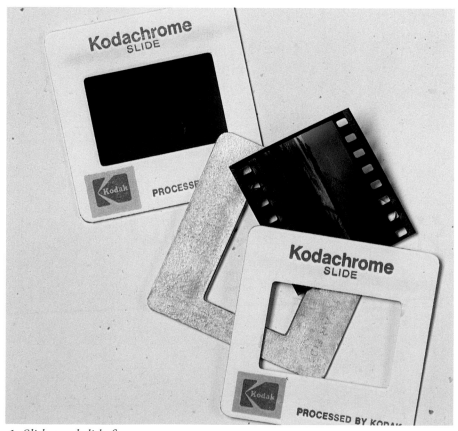

1. Slides and slide frames.

4. Squeeze out dimensional finish to cover the frame. (photo 3)

5. Sprinkle seed beads on the frame while the finish is wet. (photo 4) Let dry. (photo 5)

Assemble:

1. Position frame on print. Trace around outer edge. Cut out along the traced lines. Glue to back of frame.

2. Pierce the center top and center bottom holes again, through the paper.

3. Cut two pieces of 18 gauge wire, each 6" long. Wire wrap one end of one piece through the top hole of the frame. Wrap a loop in the other end of the wire to make a hanging loop.

4. Repeat with the other piece of wire in the bottom hole of slide. (The dangles will be attached to this loop.)

5. Make five dangles using 24 gauge wire, seed beads, and gold glass beads and wrap to bottom loop. ❑

2. Using a nail to piece a hole in the frame.

3. Squeezing dimensional finish over the paper frame.

4. Sprinkling the beads.

5. The beaded frame.

CLAY & GLASS
pendant necklace

One stunning bead that captures your fancy can be the focal point of a simple-to-make pendant necklace. Here, a polymer clay oval is combined with two glass lampwork beads.

You Will Need

Beads, Wire & Findings:

18 gauge copper wire

Oval polymer clay bead, 35mm

Round black enamel lampwork bead, 12mm

Lavender lampwork bead, 6mm

Other Supplies:

Black leather cord *or* chain

Tools:

Side cutters

Round-nose pliers

Chain-nose pliers

Measuring tape

Follow These Steps

1. Cut a piece of wire 8" long. Use the chain-nose pliers to bend an angled spiral.

2. String beads on wire:
   small lavender bead,
   black enamel bead,
   oval polymer clay bead.

3. Wire-loop above the polymer clay bead.

4. Hang on a leather cord or a chain. ❑

TURQUOISE DANGLES
pendant necklace

You can wear this pendant on a chain or a cord or on a silver neck ring, as shown here.

You Will Need

Beads, Wire & Findings:

Silver wire - 18 gauge, 24 gauge

Turquoise and green lampwork bicone bead, 20mm

Turquoise seed beads, size 11

Lime seed beads, size 11

2 turquoise bicone crystal beads, 6mm

1 oval turquoise crystal bead, 8mm

1 silver snowflake charm

Other Supplies:

Cord, neck ring, *or* chain

Tools:

Side cutters

Round-nose pliers

Chain-nose pliers

Measuring tape

Follow These Steps

1. Cut an 8" piece of 18 gauge wire. Wrap a large loop in one end. String the lampwork bead and one bicone crystal on the wire. Wrap a loop at the top of the crystal.

2. Using 24 gauge wire, make a dangle:
   silver charm wrapped at bottom,
   1" of turquoise seed beads.

3. Using 24 gauge wire, make another dangle:
   6mm bicone,
   5 turquoise seed beads,
   1 lime seed bead,
   5 turquoise seed beads,
   1 lime seed bead,
   5 turquoise seed beads.

4. Using 24 gauge wire, make another dangle:
   8mm oval crystal,
   3 turquoise seed beads and 3 lime seed beads,
   3 turquoise seed beads and 3 lime seed beads,
   3 turquoise seed beads and 3 lime seed beads,
   3 turquoise seed beads.

5. Hang on a cord, neck ring, or chain. ❑

PHOTO DECOUPAGE
pendant necklace

You can make a pendant from a favorite photo with decoupage medium, then accent it with beads. A plastic laminate sample chip from a home improvement store provides the perfect surface.

For this pendant, I used a photo of my paternal grandmother, Addie, as a young woman with two of her 10 children. Wearing her photo reminds me of the strength this small woman had all her life. I hung the first letter of her name (a piece from a Scrabble game) underneath.

You Will Need

Beads & Wire:

18 gauge silver wire
1 lampwork bead, 24mm
1 bicone crystal bead, 12mm

Other Supplies:

1 laminate sample chip
Decoupage finish, gloss
Toner photocopy of photo
Scrabble letter
Cord *or* chain
Optional: Sepia dimensional finish

Tools:

Flat paint brush
Drill and small bit
Scissors
Hole punch
Side cutters
Round-nose pliers
Chain-nose pliers

Follow These Steps

Decoupage:

1. Cut photocopy of photo to a size just a little larger than the laminate sample.

2. Brush a coat of decoupage finish on the slick side of the laminate sample. Press the photocopy to the surface. Let dry.

3. Trim edges of paper flush with laminate.

4. Brush a coat of decoupage finish over the front and edges. Let dry.

5. *Option:* Apply a coat of sepia dimensional finish. Let dry till hard.

Assemble:

1. Punch hole in paper where hole in laminate chip is.

2. Drill a small hole at bottom of chip. Drill a hole in the top of the Scrabble game piece, front to back.

Pictured left to right: Plastic laminate sample chip, vintage photo.

3. Wire letter piece to bottom of chip.

4. Cut an 8" piece of wire. Wrap to top of chip. String lampwork bead and bicone. Wrap a loop in the top.

5. Hang on a cord or chain. ❑

PLAY DOMINOS

pin

A pin with three loops (you can make it yourself using 14 gauge silver wire using the pattern below) is decorated with dangles made from beads and a domino game piece.

The back of the domino has a rubber-stamped motif. Mine is Victorian handbag design, but you can use any stamp you like. Be sure to choose an inkpad meant for use on non-porous surfaces.

You Will Need

Beads, Wire & Findings:
14 gauge silver wire
7 black crystal oval beads, 10mm
4 Bali silver tube beads, 8mm

Other Supplies:
1 "ivory" domino
Rubber stamp - Victorian purse
Black inkpad for non-porous surfaces

Tools:
Side cutters
Round-nose pliers
Chain-nose pliers
Drill and bit or drill press
Metal file
Measuring tape

Follow These Steps

Make Pin:

See the photo.

1. Cut a 12" piece of wire. Starting at the center of the wire, make a center loop by wrapping the wire around the widest part of the roundnose pliers. Repeat on either side of center loop to make other loops.

2. Following the pattern shape, bend the long end. Bend the closure end forward.

3. Trim the long wire about 1/2" past the closure.

4. Use the metal file to sharpen the end of the long wire.

Make Dangles & Assemble:

1. Stamp desired part of rubber stamp on back of domino. Let dry.

2. Cut a 6" piece of wire. Make a tiny loop in one end. String one crystal and the domino. Set aside.

3. Cut two 5" pieces of wire. Make a tiny loop in one end of each piece. String both:
crystal,
silver tube,
crystal,
silver tube,
crystal.

4. Wrap dangles to loops on pin, placing the domino on the center loop. ❑

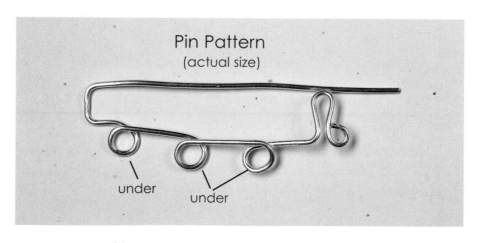

Pin Pattern
(actual size)

under

under

JAZZY JEANS
beaded chain

You can buy a hip chain or build your own hip chain by wiring two very large silver lobster clasps to the ends of a 14" big-link chain.

Assorted beads and charms.

You Will Need

Beads, Wire & Findings:

Silver hip chain, 14"

Silver wire, 18 gauge and 14 gauge

65 assorted beads and charms in a variety of types, sizes, and colors

Tools:

Side cutters

Round-nose pliers

Chain-nose pliers

Jewelry anvil

Chasing hammer

Follow These Steps

Make Hearts:

1. Using 14 gauge wire and the pattern provided, shape three wire hearts with top loops.

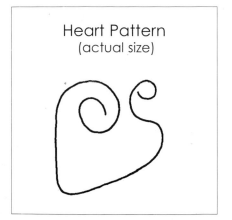

Heart Pattern
(actual size)

2. Lay on anvil and hammer flat. Tighten up the shapes and re-hammer. (Hammering the metal strengthens it.)

Assemble:

1. Using 18 gauge wire, wire wrap a bead, a combination of beads, or a charm to each link of the chain. Leave two links next to each end of the clasp without dangles.

2. Wire wrap the three flattened heart shapes where desired.

3. Hook chain to belt loops on jeans. ❏

The chain.

Hammering the metal wire.

The two hammered wire silver heart charms.

BEADS TO GO

purse handle

You Will Need

Beads, Wire & Findings:

14 gauge silver wire

6 chunks dyed coral, 25mm

4 polymer clay beads, 24mm

5 black round faceted crystal beads, 12mm

Silver chain, 2" long

Other Supplies:

Small red purse with handle loops

Tools:

Side cutters

Round-nose pliers

Measuring tape

Follow These Steps

1. Remove the handle that came with the purse.

2. Cut a piece of wire 18" long. Wrap to one purse loop.

3. String beads on wire:
   black crystal,
   coral chunk,
   polymer clay bead,
   coral chunk,
   polymer clay bead,
   black crystal,
   coral chunk,
   black crystal,
   polymer clay bead,
   coral chunk,
   polymer clay bead,
   coral chunk,
   black crystal.
   If the holes in the coral chunk beads are too narrow for the wire to fit through, use a small round file or bead reamer to gently enlarge them.

4. Wire wrap to the other purse loop.

5. Wire wrap a black crystal bead and a coral chunk to a short length of chain. Attach to zipper as a zipper pull.

Option: If the original handle of the purse was a chain, cut a short section and wire wrap the beads to it. ❑

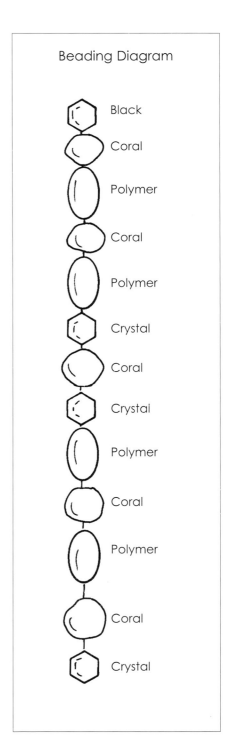

Beading Diagram

Black

Coral

Polymer

Coral

Polymer

Crystal

Coral

Crystal

Polymer

Coral

Polymer

Coral

Crystal

STITCHED
BEAD
PROJECTS

Bead fringe is easy to make and always in style
- any combination of colors and sizes of beads,
when stitched with needle and thread, will make
swingy, showy bead fringe. Bead fringe looks
good and feels good. Even if you don t sew,
it s easy to add bead fringe to a project.

You can make a lot of bead fringe in an hour - so choose your beads, thread your needle, and get busy! Use this technique to trim clothes, add pizzazz to accessories, and embellish jewelry.

Short running fringe and long fringe tassels are made the same way as bead fringe.

GLASSWORK TASSEL
necklace

You Will Need

Beads, Wire & Findings:

Beading wire, .024 diameter

Blue and green oval lampwork bead, 27mm

Seed beads, size 11 - Lime frost, lime shiny, royal blue shiny

Seed beads, size 6 - Dark green transparent

11-12 black transparent lentil crystal beads, 4mm

2 silver crimp tubes

Silver toggle clasp

Tools:

Beading needle and beading thread

Scissors

Crimping tool

Side cutters

Jewelry glue

Measuring tape

Optional: Thread wax

Follow These Steps

1. Cut twelve 1-yd. pieces of beading thread. Holding all threads together, wet or wax the ends.

2. String 15 size 8 dark green beads on each strand. Move the beads to the center of the thread. Form a loop of beads and tie a knot in all strands. See photo-you now have 24 strands of thread coming out of the loop.

3. String all 24 strands through the lampwork bead, so the loop of beads forms the hanger.

4. Place the needle on one thread. String beads:
   15 shiny lime seeds,
   11 matte lime seeds,
   10 royal blue seeds.

5. Stitch through all beads in reverse, skipping the last three royal blue beads. (This forms a triangle of beads at the bottom of the dangle - see Fig. 1.) Stitch up through lampwork bead, through hanger loop, back down through lampwork bead, and through 10-15 seed beads in the dangle. Tie a knot between seed beads, put a dot of glue on knot, trim thread.

6. Repeat the process in steps 4 and 5 to make the same dangle on each thread hanging from the lampwork bead.

Pictured at left: Loop of beads with threads.

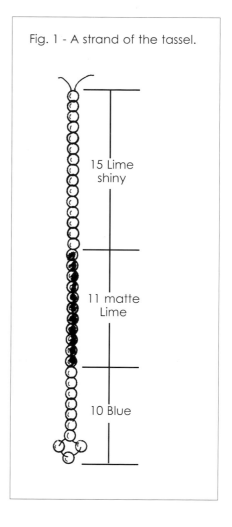

Fig. 1 - A strand of the tassel.

15 Lime shiny

11 matte Lime

10 Blue

7. String dark green beads and crystal beads on wire to desired length, placing a crystal between each group of 10 dark green beads.

8. Crimp toggle clasp pieces on ends.

9. Slide beaded tassel on necklace. ❑

AUTUMN FRINGE
embellished scarf

You Will Need

Beads:

Rust seed beads, size 11

Bronze seed beads, size 8

Gold twisted bugle beads

Fabric:

Sheer fabric in autumnal neutral
colors, 54" x 14"

Tools:

Beading needle and thread

Scissors

Iron

Jewelry glue

Optional: Sewing machine, thread
wax

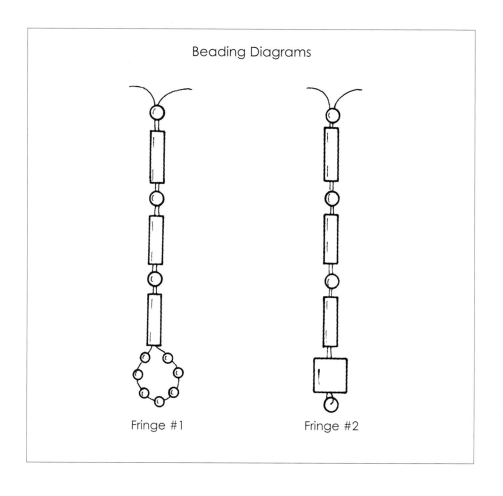

Beading Diagrams

Fringe #1   Fringe #2

Follow These Steps

1. Hem all sides of fabric with a
rolled hem done either by hand or
on the sewing machine to make a
scarf. Press flat.

2. Thread needle. Alternately stitch
Fringe 1 and Fringe 2 (see below)
across both ends. Place dangles
1/4" apart.

• Fringe 1:
1 rust seed bead,
bugle bead,
1 rust seed bead,
bugle bead,
1 rust seed bead,
bugle bead,
7 rust seed beads.
Stitch through beads in reverse,
skipping the bottom seven beads.
(They make a circle of beads at
the end of the dangle.)

• Fringe 2:
1 rust seed bead,
bugle bead,
1 rust seed bead,
bugle bead,
1 rust seed bead,
bugle bead,
1 bronze seed bead,
1 rust seed bead.
Stitch through beads in reverse,
skipping the last seed bead.

3. Tie off threads at end. ❏

FASHIONABLE FRINGE
embellished sweater

Beading the neckline of a sweater creates a very special necklace that fits and hangs just right. Here, I've used leaf beads on a pale green sweater. You could use warm bead colors to embellish a fall sweater, or use small flower beads instead of leaf beads.

You Will Need

Beads:

Iridescent aqua seed beads, size 11

15 blue-green glass leaf beads, 10mm long

Other Supplies:

Lime green sweater

Tools:

Beading needle and thread

Scissors

Jewelry glue

Optional: Thread wax

Follow These Steps

1. Locate center of neckline. Thread needle and, at center, stitch from inside of sweater to front.

2. String beads for dangle:
   15 seed beads,
   leaf bead.

3. Stitch back through the bottom five seed beads.

4. Add four seed beads. Stitch back through three beads, skipping the first bead.

5. Stitch back through five beads.

6. Add four seed beads. Stitch back through three beads, skipping the first bead.

7. Stitch back through the last five beads. Stitch through sweater to inside and tie off thread.

8. Repeat the process to make 15 dangles 3/4" apart. After every two dangles, knot and cut thread. (This keeps the neckline of the sweater stretchable, so it will fit over your head.)

To wash: Turn sweater inside out and wash by hand. ❏

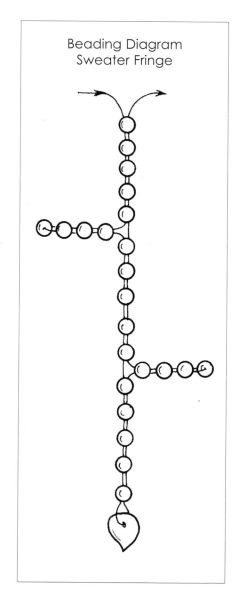

Beading Diagram
Sweater Fringe

Ideas for Dangles

Long Dangles

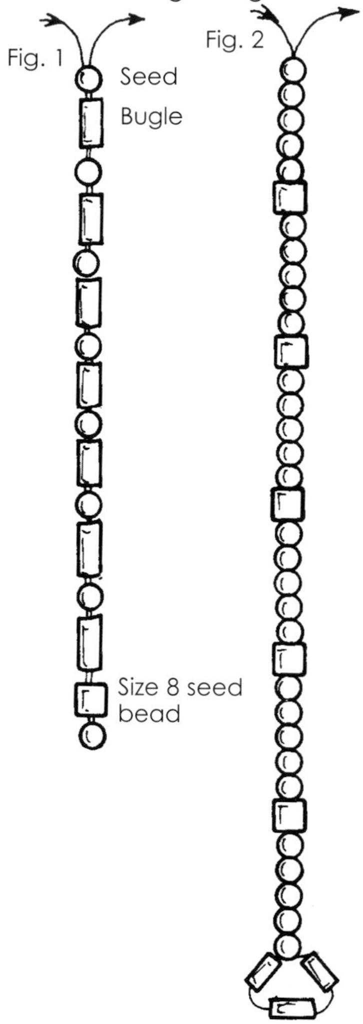

Fig. 1
Seed
Bugle

Size 8 seed bead

Fig. 2

Medium Dangles

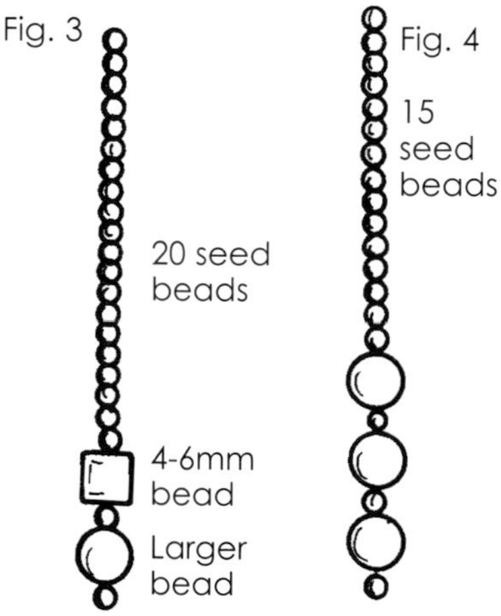

Fig. 3
20 seed beads
4-6mm bead
Larger bead

Fig. 4
15 seed beads

Short Dangles

Fig. 5   Fig. 6

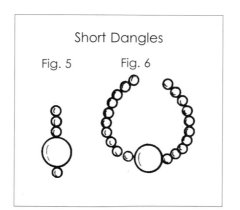

CHARMED FRINGE

purse

This simple purse is made from an upholstery remnant. I chose beads to match the purse fabric and had fun selecting a variety of charms to adorn the fringe. I used a curtain tie-back (find them in the drapery notions departments of fabric stores) as a strap.

You Will Need:

Beads, Wire & Findings:
Seed beads, size 11
Variety of beads in all sizes and shapes
Silver charms
Old skeleton key

Other Supplies:
1 yd. upholstery fabric, at least 36" wide
Curtain tie-back cord

Tools:
Beading needle and thread
Scissors
Iron
Pencil
Jewelry glue
Optional: Sewing machine, thread wax

Follow These Steps

Construct Purse:

1. Cut two rectangles fabric, each 14" x 30".

2. Cut one end to a point or any other shape you would like the front flap to be.

3. With right sides facing, stitch pieces together, leaving a 5" opening for turning.

4. Turn, trim seams, hand stitch opening, and press flat.

5. Fold the straight end up 10". Make a pencil line on the bottom fold on the outside of the purse.

Add Fringe & Finish:

Use the dangle ideas provided or make up your own.

1. Thread needle. Make fringe dangles along the marked line, adding charms to some dangles. Stitch skeleton key as a dangle.

2. Stitch sides of purse together.

3. Fold flap over purse.

4. Stitch curtain tie-back in place to form the strap.

5. Add seven dangles to the flap. ❏

COMBINATION OF TECHNIQUES

Stringing, wire wrapping, and stitching are
great beading techniques on their own.
Once you start to think about combinations, the
possibilities are endless.

Stringing seed beads makes a fast and
easy base for a bead fringe bracelet
or necklace. Adding a wire-wrapped dangle
or charm to any piece makes it unique.
Enjoy the possibilities!

MARTINI NIGHT

bracelet

This bracelet takes its inspiration from the colors
of the pimento-stuffed olive.

You Will Need

Beads, Wire & Findings:

Beading wire, .024

Green matte seed beads, size 6

Red matte seed beads, size 8

Red seed beads, size 11

Red beads, various types, 3mm

6 green glass olive beads, 18mm

4 round red faceted crystal beads, 10mm

Silver decorative clasp

2 silver crimp tubes

18 gauge silver wire

Martini charm (glass *or* metal)

Tools:

Side cutters

Beading needle and thread

Scissors

Crimping tool

Round-nose pliers

Chain-nose pliers

Jewelry glue

Optional: Thread wax

Follow These Steps

Note: A "small red bead" can be a size 8 seed bead, a size 11 seed bead, or a 3mm bead.

1. String size 8 red seed beads to length desired with toggle clasp attached. Crimp toggle clasp pieces to ends.

2. Thread needle. Starting at one end of the bracelet, stitch a fringe dangle after each bead, all the way to the end of the bracelet. To make the fringe dangle, string 5 green seed beads and finish with *either* 1 small red bead and 1 red size 11 seed bead *or* 3 red size 11 seed beads.

3. Working from the other end of bracelet back to the starting point, stitch a fringe dangle of 4 green seed beads after each bead.

4. Working from starting point to the other end, stitch a fringe dangle after each bead made from 3 green seed beads and 1 small red bead.

5. Add 5 olive bead dangles, spacing them evenly along the bracelet. To make the dangle, string:
   1 green seed bead,
   1 olive bead,
   1 small red bead.

6. Add four red crystal dangles between the olive dangles. To make the dangle, string:
   1 red seed bead,
   1 red crystal,
   1 red seed bead.

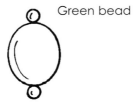

Beading Diagrams

Olive Bead Dangle

Green bead

Red Crystal Bead Dangle

7. Wire wrap remaining olive bead to the loop of the open end of the toggle clasp.

8. Wire wrap martini charm to the same loop. ❑

FRINGE & FIBERS
Bracelet

You Will Need

Beads, Wire, & Findings:

Beading wire, .024

Blue and yellow lampwork cylinder bead, 30mm

Two colors of blue seed beads, size 11

Blue cube seed beads, size 8

About 40 assorted small blue and yellow beads, 3mm or 4mm, plus size 8 seed beads

2 silver crimp beads

Decorative silver toggle clasp

Other Supplies:

Blue fuzzy fibers or yarn

Tools:

Side cutters

Crimping tool

Scissors

Beading needle and thread

Jewelry glue

Optional: Thread wax

Follow These Steps

1. String a bracelet with cube beads, stringing the lampwork bead in the center. Adjust the length to fit the wrist with the length of the toggle clasp included. Crimp toggle clasp pieces to ends of bracelet.

2. Thread needle. Working from one end of the bracelet to the other, stitch a fringe dangle after each cube bead. To make the fringe dangle, string:

6 blue seed beads,
1 larger bead,
1 seed bead.

3. Working from end of bracelet back to the starting point, stitch a fringe dangle after each cube bead. To make the dangle, string:
4 seed beads,
1 larger bead,

1 seed bead.

4. Cut a 4" piece of fiber. Tie and knot between two cube beads. Trim ends of fiber so they are slightly longer than the bead fringe. Repeat the process to make six fiber ties on each side of the bracelet. ❏

LONG FRINGE

ankle bracelet

You Will Need

Beads, Wire & Findings:

Beading wire, .024

21 lavender oval faceted crystal beads, 5mm

24 round Bali silver spacer beads, 4mm

70 Bali silver barrel beads, 3mm

2 silver crimp tubes

Silver lobster clasp

Tools:

Side cutters

Crimping tool

Beading needle and thread

Jewelry glue

Measuring tape

Optional: Thread wax

Follow These Steps

1. Cut beading wire 2" longer than ankle measurement.

2. Crimp lobster clasp to one end of wire.

3. String:
   crystal,
   round bali,
   barrel bali,
   round bali.
   Repeat until the anklet fits around the ankle.

4. Crimp the end with a loop in the wire.

5. Thread needle. Stitch five or six

dangles, graduating from 1" to 2-1/2" long, at the center of the anklet with barrel beads and a crystal. ❑

EVENING OUT
purse strap embellishment

This black bag is anything but basic! A variety of black beads (a mixture I like to call "bead soup") adds sparkle and pizzazz to this pouch purse. I attached it with lanyard clips, which make it easy to remove, but you could stitch the new strap and the dangles directly to the bag instead of using the clips.

You Will Need

Beads, Wire & Findings:

Beading wire, .019

2 silver crimp tubes

Black opal bugle beads

A variety of black beads, all shapes and sizes

2 black lampwork cylinder bead, 44mm

2 silver lanyard clips

20 gauge silver wire

Other Supplies:

Small black purse or pouch

Tools:

Crimping tool

Side cutters

Round-nose pliers

Chain-nose pliers

Jewelry glue

Measuring tape

Optional: Thread wax

Follow These Steps

1. Remove strap from purse. If the purse doesn't have loops for attaching a strap, make two loops from the old strap and sew them to the bag.

2. Attach the lanyard clips to the loops.

3. Cut two lengths of beading wire 2" longer than you want the straps to be. Crimp one end of each wire to one lanyard clip.

4. String both wires with bugle beads, adding in some smaller black beads. Every few inches, string both wires through a single bead or group of three beads (Fig. 1). When the wires are full, crimp the ends to the other lanyard clip.

5. Cut a 6" piece of silver wire. Holding one end tightly with the roundnose pliers, bend into a spiral. String the lampwork bead and add various black beads to make a dangle 4-5" long. Wrap to one lanyard clip.

6. Make two more dangles, each a little shorter. Wrap to the same lanyard clip. ❏

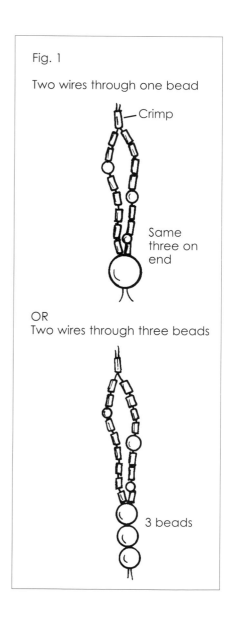

Fig. 1

Two wires through one bead

Crimp

Same three on end

OR

Two wires through three beads

3 beads

BEADED SHOULDERS
camisole straps

Beaded straps with flower dangles dress up a simple cotton camisole. These straps are attached with crimp tubes. If you like, you can make the straps removable by attaching lobster clasps to the ends - you can hook the lobster clasps to the strap loops and unhook them as needed. Having removable straps would allow machine washing.

You Will Need

Beads, Wire & Findings:

Beading wire, .024

Seed beads, size 11 - Deep plum, dark leaf green, medium blue

Seed beads, size 6 - Dark leaf green

4 silver crimp tubes

Other Supplies:

Black camisole

Tools:

Beading needle and thread

Crimping tool

Side cutters

Jewelry glue

Scissors

Measuring tape

Black sewing thread and needle

Optional: Thread wax

Follow These Steps

1. Cut each end of camisole straps 1/2" above body of tank. Fold one 1/2" strap piece to the inside and stitch in place, forming a loop. Repeat for other three strap ends.

2. Cut wire 2" longer than desired length of finished strap. Run through front strap loop and crimp.

3. String size 6 green seed beads to the strap length, stringing the beads so they are a bit loose. (This allows the strap to move with the body and allows room to stitch between beads.) Crimp to back strap loop.

4. Thread needle and tie to last green bead on wire. Stitch a flower dangle using one color seed beads for "petals" and the other color for the center. (See Fig. 1) Stitch through the next three beads on the wire, then stitch another dangle, reversing the colors. Continue along the strap, adding a flower dangle every three

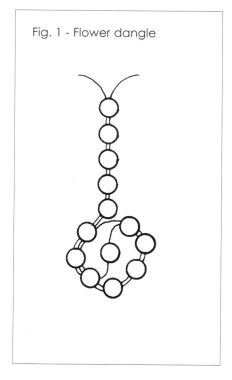

Fig. 1 - Flower dangle

beads. Tie off thread, knot, and trim.

5. Repeat the process on the other strap.

To wash: Hand wash and line dry. ❏

GARDEN GREENS

necklace

Fig. 1 - 25-bead dangles

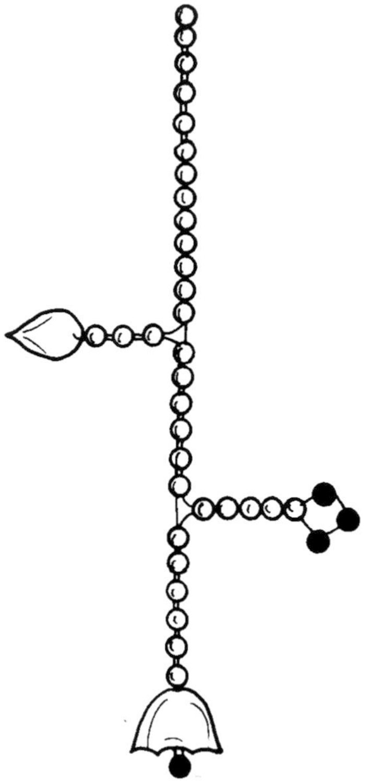

Garden-theme beads are strung at the ends of seed bead fringe to create the full, lush look of this necklace.

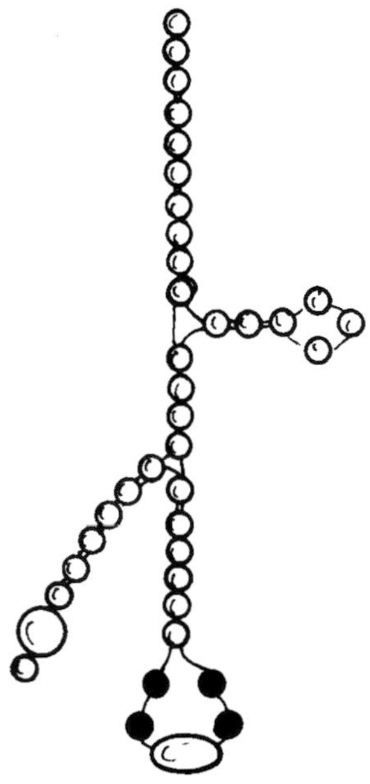

You Will Need

Beads, Wire & Findings:

Beading wire, .024

Green seed bead mix, size 6 (all colors and finishes of greens)

Green seed bead mix, size 11 (all colors and finishes of greens)

"Bead soup" - Seed beads, larger glass beads, flower beads, and leaf beads

Silver lobster clasp and split ring

2 silver crimp tubes

Tools:

Beading needle and thread

Scissors

Crimping tool

Jewelry glue

Measuring tape

Optional: Thread wax

Follow These Steps

String:

1. Cut a 24" piece of wire. Crimp lobster clasp to one end.
2. Loosely string wire with size 6 green beads.
3. Crimp split ring to other end.

Add Dangles:

Each dangle is made of seed beads and decorated at the end with a bead or beads from the "bead soup." See Fig. 5 for examples of dangle ends.

1. Thread needle. Starting in the center of the necklace, make a dangle 25 seed beads long. (Fig. 1)
2. Stitch one base bead over. Make another dangle 25 seed beads long. Repeat three more times for a total of five, stitching along the base.

Continued on page 124

Fig. 2 - 20-bead dangles

Fig. 3 - 15-bead dangles

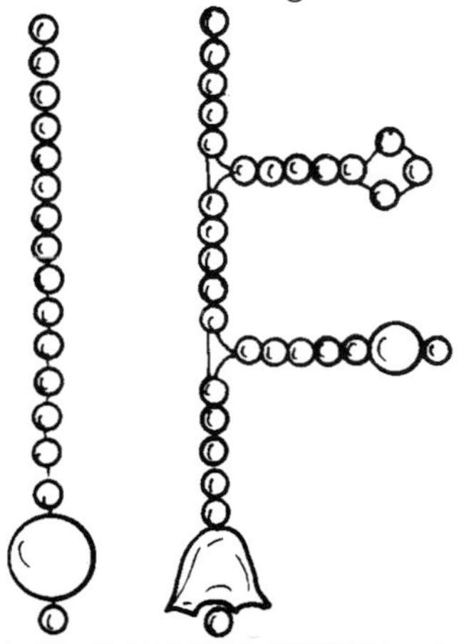

Fig. 4 - 10-bead dangles

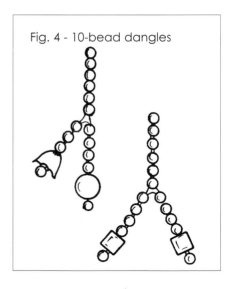

Continued from page 122

3. Stitch eight dangles 20 seed beads long. (Fig. 2)
4. Stitch eight dangles 15 seed beads long. (Fig. 3)
5. Stitch eight dangles 10 seed beads long. (Fig. 4)
6. Stitch eight dangles 5 seed beads long.
7. Repeat steps 2 through 5, working in the other direction from the center.
8. Repeat, working your way across the necklace base two more times, adding dangle fringe after each base bead.
9. Make two more passes across the base necklace, stitching dangles of 5 to 10 seed beads only. (This adds volume to the fringe.) ❑

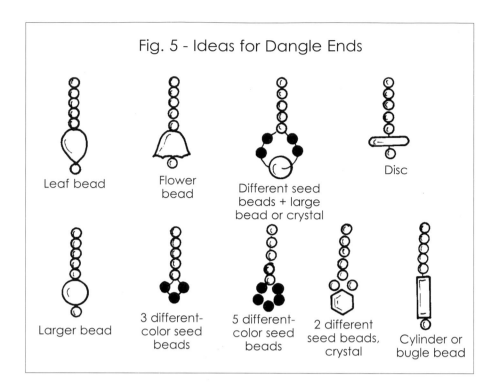

Fig. 5 - Ideas for Dangle Ends

Leaf bead

Flower bead

Different seed beads + large bead or crystal

Disc

Larger bead

3 different-color seed beads

5 different-color seed beads

2 different seed beads, crystal

Cylinder or bugle bead

CRYSTAL LADDER
bracelet

Two rails of cube beads are joined by rungs of seed beads, silver flowers, and faceted crystals to make this ladder.

You Will Need

Beads, Wire & Findings:

Beading wire, .024

50 turquoise crystal cube beads, 4mm cube

50 blue crystal cube beads, 4mm

Turquoise seed beads, size 11

Blue seed beads, size 11

5 aqua round faceted crystal beads, 10mm

5 light blue bicone faceted crystal beads, 10mm

9 silver metal flower beads, 5mm

4 silver crimp tubes

Tools:

Side cutters

Crimping tool

Beading needle and thread

Jewelry glue

Measuring tape

Optional: Thread wax

Follow These Steps

String:

1. Cut two pieces of beading wire, each 15" long.

2. About 4" from one end, crimp a tube on the wire.

3. String cube beads, alternating colors, to the length of your wrist measurement minus 1". Crimp another tube at the end of the beads so the beads are not tight on the wire. See photo.

4. Repeat on the other wire exactly.

Add Dangles:

Always skip two cube beads between dangles.

1. Thread needle. Tie on between first and second cube bead on one wire.

2. Stitch dangle:
   3 seed beads,
   1 crystal bead,
   3 seeds.

3. Stitch into second cube bead on other wire. Stitch through two cube beads.

4. Stitch second dangle:
   6 seed beads,
   flower bead,
   2 seed beads.

5. Stitch into third bead from the first dangle. Stitch through two cube beads.

6. Stitch the third dangle the same as the first, but use a different crystal bead and the other color seed beads. Skip two cube beads on the other side, stitch through two.

7. Make fourth dangle:
   2 seed beads,
   flower bead,
   6 seed beads.

8. Repeat the sequence from dangle one until you have just one cube bead left on each wire. Pull thread snugly.

Finish the End:

1. String three cube beads on each wire.

2. String both wires through a crimp tube and a cube bead. Crimp toggle clasp piece to end.

3. Repeat on the other end. Try on the bracelet and adjust for fit. Add or subtract cubes to make the bracelet the right length. ❏

You Will Need

Beads, Wire & Findings:

3 polymer clay face beads, 28mm

"Bead soup" of size 11 seed beads -
 Yellow, orange, red

Matte brass seed beads, size 8

18 gauge copper wire

16 gauge copper wire

Tools:

Beading needle and thread

Side cutters

Round-nose pliers

Chain-nose pliers

Jewelry glue

Optional: Thread wax

Follow These Steps

1. Thread needle. Stitch through face bead. String enough seed beads to fit across top of head. Knot threads together so the beads run across the top of the head. (Fig. 1)
2. Stitch seed bead dangles between the beads running across the head. Make dangles short at the sides (3 beads), graduating the length so they are longer (9 beads) at the center of the head. (Fig. 2)
3. Work back the other way, making a second set of dangles. Pull thread tight, knot, and glue knot.
4. Repeat for two more face beads.
5. Cut a 4" piece of wire. Wire wrap both ends so the loops are close to the head. Cut another piece of wire. Wrap to the right loop of the first face.
6. Slide another head on the wire. Wrap a loop close to the head on the other side.

FAMILIAR FACES
necklace

Beaded fringe creates hair for three clay face beads.

7. Repeat for the third face bead.
8. Wrap and attach links made of nine matte brass beads on both sides until necklace is desired length.
9. Make a toggle clasp from copper wire and attach it to the necklace. ❑

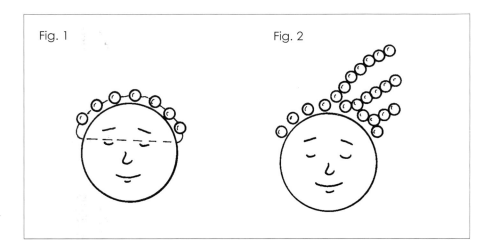

Fig. 1

Fig. 2

METRIC CONVERSION CHART

Inches to Millimeters and Centimeters

Inches	MM	CM
1/8	3	.3
1/4	6	.6
3/8	10	1.0
1/2	13	1.3
5/8	16	1.6
3/4	19	1.9
7/8	22	2.2
1	25	2.5
1-1/4	32	3.2
1-1/2	38	3.8
1-3/4	44	4.4
2	51	5.1
3	76	7.6
4	102	10.2
5	127	12.7
6	152	15.2
7	178	17.8
8	203	20.3
9	229	22.9
10	254	25.4
11	279	27.9
12	305	30.5

Yards to Meters

Yards	Meters
1/8	.11
1/4	.23
3/8	.34
1/2	.46
5/8	.57
3/4	.69
7/8	.80
1	.91
2	1.83
3	2.74
4	3.66
5	4.57
6	5.49
7	6.40
8	7.32
9	8.23
10	9.14

INDEX